WEAVING Rag Rugs

WEAVING
Rag Rugs

TOM KNISELY

STACKPOLE
BOOKS

Published by
STACKPOLE BOOKS
5067 Ritter Road
Mechanicsburg, PA 17055
www.stackpolebooks.com

Printed in U.S.A.

First edition

Cover design by Wendy Reynolds
Photography by Impact Xpozures

Library of Congress Cataloging-in-Publication Data

Knisely, Tom.
Weaving rag rugs / Tom Knisely. — First edition.
pages cm
Includes bibliographical references.
ISBN 978-0-8117-1212-5
1. Rag rugs. 2. Hand weaving—Patterns. I. Title.

TT850.K627 2014
746.7'041—dc23

2013036398

With Heartfelt Dedication

I would like to dedicate this book to all those weavers of rag rugs who left behind so many wonderful examples of their work for me to discover and to study.

I'm sure they never considered their rag rugs to be works of art. Their resourcefulness, frugality, and creative ways are evident in each one of these old rag rugs. I am positive that their intent was to make a meager living at weaving or at least contribute to the family's income. I wonder if they thought about the little bits of torn fabric as they wove them into the rug. Did they think about these thin little contributions and remember where the fabric originally started out? Maybe they remembered that strip from the children's play clothes and this piece from Grandma's old apron—but most likely they simply had a rug to weave, and dozens more after that. There was a job to do and they did it. I can promise you that they didn't think about me a hundred years in the future looking closely at their rugs and studying them and romantically making up stories in my mind about those little thin strips of fabric.

I am indebted to all these old weavers who have taught me through their work to have pride in what you weave and to make a quality product that will last for years—just as their rugs have. I hope that someday, someone will look at my work and wonder, if only for a moment, about the weaver who created the piece. I would like to think we all hope for this.

There is a wonderful saying that you sometimes find cross-stitched on old samplers and show towels that goes like this: "When I am dead and in my grave and all my bones are rotten, when this you see, remember me, lest I be forgotten." A little morbid, don't you think? But just the same, a valuable quote to remember as you weave your own rag rug. Weave it with pride and weave it to last.

Happy weaving!

Contents

Introduction

I bought my first loom in 1976. It was a massive loom with two harness frames. Although my patterning possibilities were limited, it still allowed me to weave plain weave and I spent the next few months thinking about all the different ways that I could weave and make patterns with just two harness. Of course, 1976 was the bicentennial of our country and this united with my natural interest in history to raise my interest in anything remotely related to things "Old Timey." Perhaps that is why I bought that huge antique barn frame loom rather than something of a more reasonable size for my home. In any event, it proved to be the right choice. When I discovered rag rugs, I had just the right loom to start weaving them on.

When you weave a rag rug, you join in a tradition that dates back over a hundred years. When exactly rag weaving began is unknown, but many believe it started in several places around the world, most likely during the late eighteenth or early nineteenth century. The practice began in part because of the industrial revolution and the introduction of machine-woven cotton fabric. Prior to this period,

Typical hit-and-miss rag rug from the early twentieth century

hand-woven fabric was a precious commodity, and people didn't have extra rags to tear up and weave into rugs. Even old, threadbare fabric would find a use somewhere else in the home: A large bed sheet with a hole would become a pillow case; worn-out pillow cases would be used as cleaning rags or to patch other fabrics. But with the invention of mechanical looms, fabric became much cheaper and quicker to make, and common people, for the first time, had fabric to spare for weaving into floor coverings.

Fairly early on, merchants in the Americas were offering strips of brightly colored warp-face carpeting with bold stripes and some simple color and weave effects such as log cabin patterns. They were woven as plain weave on just two shafts and went by the name "Venetian Carpets." (The carpeting was imported from England and had nothing to do with the city of Venice, Italy.) It didn't take long for American weavers to see the popularity of this type of carpeting, so they started weaving variations of this Venetian carpet. Weavers would take out advertisements in local newspapers offering their services to weave "fancy coverlets" or carpets.

In the later part of the nineteenth century, when the popularity of the coverlet started to decrease, weavers continued to weave rag carpets to keep their doors open. The weaver would provide the warp, and the customer would bring the weft for the rug, with the rags already cut into strips and sewn together. The weaver would have designed his or her own patterns for the rug's warp. These might be a simple plain colored cotton warp or an alternating light and dark colored warp. The later arrangement is known as log cabin and produces short horizontal dashes of dark and light colors.

When homeowners were ready to have new carpeting made, they would invite their community to come to their home for a carpet party. Rags and clothing that had been saved for years would be brought out and the guests attending the party would cut them into strips, sew the strips together, and wind them into balls. Those sewing the strips

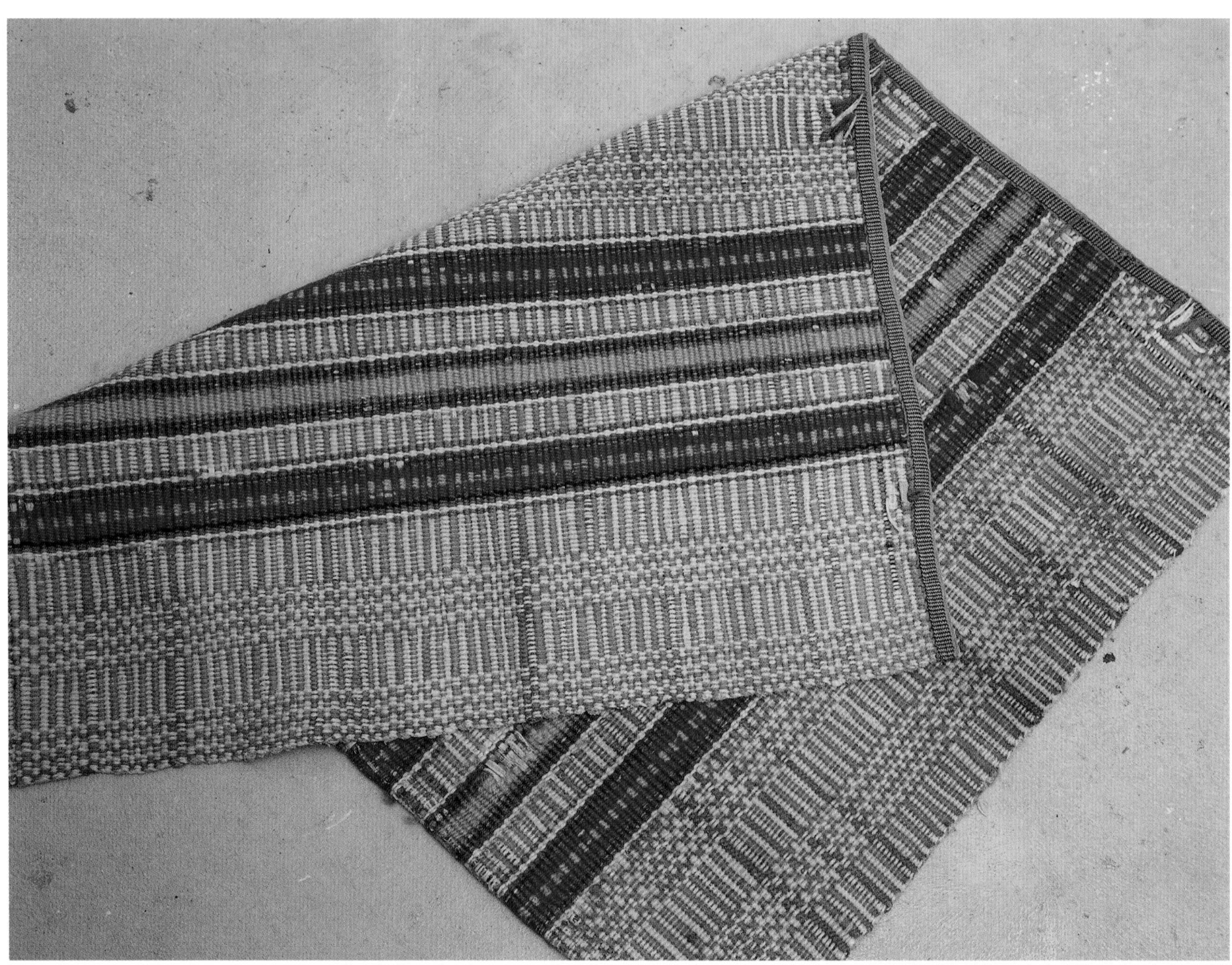

Late-nineteenth-century Venetian carpet

Early-twentieth-century Japanese *obis* made using the *sakiori* technique

together were careful to mix up the colors of the fabric, avoiding having too many strips of the same color sewn together, which would result in large pools of a single color in the rug. This attractive style of alternating the colors randomly, mixing darks with lights, is now refered to as a "hit-and-miss" rag rug.

Rag rugs were also very popular throughout Scandinavia in the mid-nineteenth century—and in such a cold climate it's not hard to imagine why. I have seen photographs of nineteenth-century Scandinavian homes where rag rugs were laid close together and on top of each other to keep the drafts from coming up between the floorboards. A popular style of rag rugs from this period was *ripsmatta*; these rugs used bold geometric patterns with diamond and circle motifs, resembling coverlet patterns. These rugs were most likely woven by professional weavers, not by rural home weavers.

Around the same time in Japan, weavers were recycling cotton rags in a slightly different way. For many years, peasant farmers and coastal fisherman and their families wore clothing woven from bast fiber such as hemp, nettle, and the processed inner bark of trees. Around the mid- to late nineteenth century, rag merchants began to sell worn-out pieces of cotton fabric in the countryside. Rural weavers began to use strips of cotton fabric ¼ to ⅓ inch wide as weft in hemp or other bast fiber warp. Using only two-shaft looms and weaving in plain weave, they produced a fabric that was not only much softer to the touch than the bast fabric they had been wearing, but also quite durable. This technique, known as *sakiori,* immediately became a popular way of weaving fabric for clothing. *Sakiori* was woven on narrow warps sometimes only twelve inches wide. In later years and even today, weavers have taken *sakiori* to a whole new level, weaving narrow strips of fabric that can only be described as works of art. Today, *sakiori* is highly sought after by textile collectors and decorators to use as art fabrics for wall hangings and pillows.

I will warn you right now that weaving rag rugs is addictive. When I started out, I learned something new with each rug I wove. I learned that by changing the colors of the warp threads and arranging the colors in stripes I could add beauty and variations to this humble textile and push it forward in a new direction. I was having the time of my life discovering all the possibilities of weaving these simple rag rugs—and I have spent decades now enjoying weaving them. My hope is that you will have as much fun as I do in this craft—and in your connection to the hundreds of weavers in the past who supplemented their income by weaving rag rugs in their community.

CHAPTER 1

The Loom and Other Tools

When weaving rag rugs—or any other heavy textile—you need to be mindful of the fact that you are asking oversized materials to be tightly interwoven together to make a solid, hard-wearing item. Rag rugs need to be woven on sturdy looms that will withstand heavy beating; much of the other equipment that you use also needs to be extra strong to handle the challenge of a rag rug. Let's take a look at all the things you will need to make a great rag rug.

Loom

It's easy to get excited about weaving a rag rug and forget to make sure you have a suitable loom to weave it on. Your loom needs to be heavy, sturdy, and very strong. When looking over a loom, make sure that the frame is made of thick and heavy timbers, with tight joints where the pieces come together. This will add to the overall strength.

Most floor looms are fine to weave a rag rug on; the heavier the loom, the better the final results. A portable floor

High-castle jack loom

loom that can fold up for easier moving is not a good choice for weaving rugs. Each spot on the loom that folds is a weak spot, and every weak spot compromises the overall sturdiness of the loom. Smaller portable looms and table top looms will work for other types of rag weaving (such as rag placemats, table runners, and and lightweight textiles such as Japanese *sakiori* fabric), but for a rug you really want a solidly built floor loom.

Before you start your rug, go over the loom and tighten the nuts and bolts or tap in the wedges that hold the frame together.

Weighting the beater of your loom is great trick to help you beat the rags into the web of your rug. There are numerous ways to do this, but the one that I think works the best is to simply attach a heavy steel bar to the underside of the beater. I went to a local welding shop and told the owner what my intentions were and they fixed me up with a piece of steel that was about 3/8 of an inch thick and 2 1/2 inches wide. They cut this piece to a length that just fit between the uprights of the beater and drilled holes several inches apart down the length of the bar. All I had to do was screw the bar to the beater. The steel bar added about 10 pounds to the beater. At first I was concerned that the added weight would have to be removed when I wasn't weaving rugs, but I got used to the weight of the beater and for textiles and fabrics that require a lighter beat I simply pull my punches and don't beat as hard.

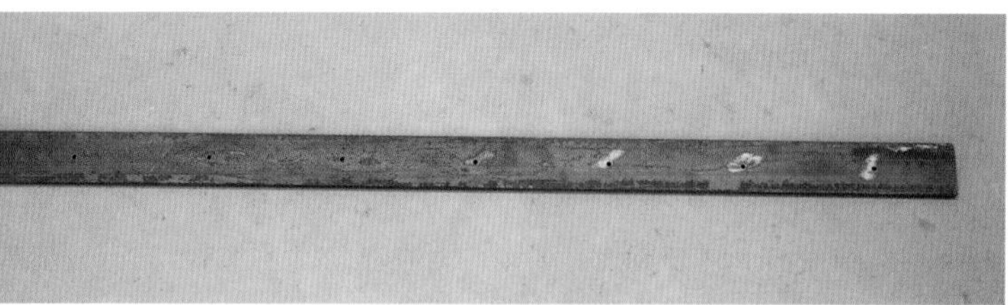
A steel bar for weighting the beater

Brace your loom with wood blocks

You may want to ask your loom manufacturer if they offer a weighted beater for the loom. If you can order the weights directly from the manufacturer, it could save you a lot of time.

Another good way to prep your loom for the heavy work of rug making is to brace the front uprights to prevent the loom from sliding forward as you beat. To do this, simply cut two pieces of heavy wood to a length that allows you to place them between the front uprights and an outside wall of your weaving studio. They should be about 27 to 30 inches long so as to give you enough space to place your bench between the wall and the loom. Make sure there is a thick and tall baseboard on the outside wall—or even better, brace your loom against a concrete block wall. You don't want to drive the supports through the wall!

When selecting a loom to weave rag rugs, you also want to think about the shedding action. There are three types of looms to consider. Jack looms have a shedding system that raises the shafts. There are also counterbalance looms and countermarch looms, in which the shafts move in opposite directions. The two latter types of looms are generally preferred by rug weavers the world over because of the increased shed opening. This makes it easier to work with large shuttles wound with bulky materials. With the jack loom, the warp threads lie on the shuttle race of the beater and are at their lowest position when the shed is being opened. The warp needs to be kept tight for rag rug weaving, but if it is too tight, it can be difficult to achieve a shed that allows for easy weaving. If you are weaving on a jack loom you might need to decrease the tension on the warp slightly to get a great shed. With the counterbalance or countermarch loom the tight warp threads pass through the loom's reed above the shuttle race at a distance about a third the height of the reed. The warp moves both up and down, creating a larger shed than can be achieved on a jack loom, where the warp only goes up.

The counterbalance loom works well as a two- or four-shaft loom, but the countermarch loom, with its more complex tie-up, can easily weave as an eight-, ten-, sixteen-, or twenty-shaft loom. However, there are very few instances in weaving rag rugs where an eight-shaft loom is required. Warp-face rep weave is an exception, as with this type of weaving, the designs become crisper and more complex the more shafts you use. The majority of rag rugs can be woven on four or fewer shafts; many are woven as a simple plain weave.

Another important consideration is the type of heddle on your loom. Heddles with small eyes are more difficult to

Jack loom

Countermarch loom

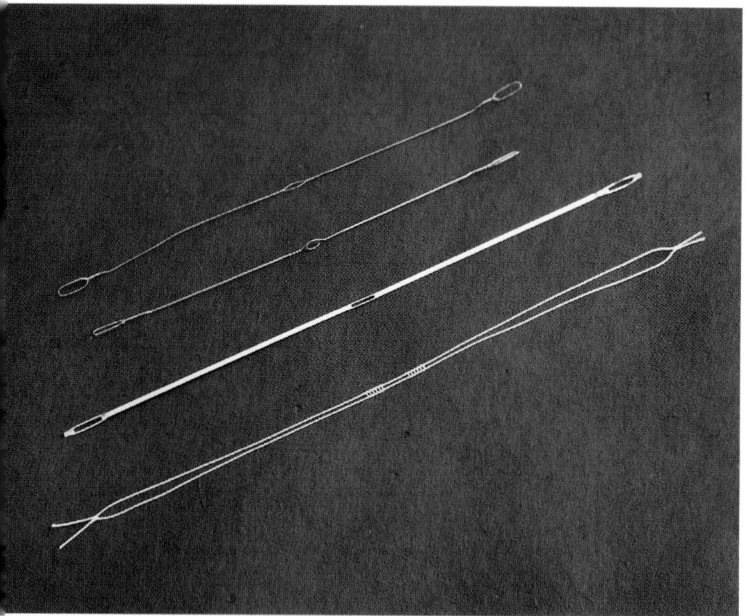
Heddles

thread and also present a chaffing problem for thicker warp threads. Inserted eye heddles and nylon heddles are good choices for rug weaving as they allow the warp threads to pass through more easily. The nylon heddles are very flexible and may be slightly slower to thread than the wire heddles with the inserted eye. I prefer the inserted eye heddles on a shaft with a solid frame and the nylon heddles on Scandinavian-style looms that have wooden heddle bars only on the top and bottom of the shaft.

The loom will have either a flat warp beam or a sectional warp beam (easily recognized by the wooden or metal pins that extend outward from the beam and divide the beam into one- or two-inch sections). The flat warp beam is more common. When you wind the warp onto this beam you will need to separate the layers with heavy paper, single-face corrugated paper, or the tried-and-true method used for centuries, wooden slats. The wooden slats are inserted into the warp with each turn of the beam. Several slats per turn is not excessive as this helps to keep the warp under even tension. If

Counterbalance loom with sectional beam

Corrugated paper wound between the layers of warp

you are using heavy paper or corrugated paper, feed it into the warp as you wind the warp onto the warp beam to separate the layers. Without the wooden slats or paper, the warp will collapse under the tension put on it when weaving.

The sectional warp beam, with its dividers, doesn't require paper or slats because the pegs extending out from the warp beam support the warp threads, preventing them from spreading and collapsing under the warp's tension. With this kind of warp beam, the warp is wound one section at a time. See chapter 4 for more on warping this kind of warp beam.

Shuttles

The rag rug weaver's shuttles are larger than the boat shuttles used for fabric weaving. They need to be able to hold large amounts of rags so that the weaver can weave several inches

A sectional warp beam

Rag shuttle

Ski shuttle

Rug shuttle

of the rug before having to join a new end. Rag shuttles remind me of a catamaran boat: They have two smoothly finished side boards turned on end and held together with two or three crosspieces. The space between the side boards measures between 1½ and 2 inches. This allows you to wind several yards of rags flatly, without folding or twisting, around the middle of the shuttle.

Ski shuttles resemble a ski with two turned up ends. A board attached perpendicularly to the flat side of the ski holds the rags. With each of these shuttles you need to wind the rags onto the shuttle by hand and then unwind the rags by a few turns before you throw the shuttle. The process may seem very awkward at first, but remember that rag rugs weave up very quickly.

In the beginning and ending portion of each rag rug, a heading needs to be woven to secure the rags. This is usually woven with a conventional boat shuttle.

Temple

This tool is known by several names—"temple," "tenterhook," and "stretcher"—and is a device that keeps the selvedges from pulling in. The temple is made of wood or metal and slides much like a slide rule to adjust to several weaving widths. At the ends there are sharp stainless-steel teeth that, when inserted into the meaty part of the rug, help to prevent the edges from naturally pulling in. Place the temple into the rug as soon as possible, adjusting it to the width of the warp as it is in the reed. As you weave your rug, move the temple every 1½ to 2 inches for the length of the rug. This doesn't prevent the rug from ultimately drawing in but does keep it pulled out to the weaving width when the beater and reed strike the fell of your rug.

Wood and metal temples

Scissors, Rag Cutters, and Rotary Cutters

Treat yourself to a great pair of scissors that are made of good quality materials. Gingher and Fisker, as well as some other manufacturers, are good choices to pick for your weaving studio. Keep them away from the kitchen drawer, craft drawer, and most of all from other members of the family who might mistake them for just another pair of scissors and use them for cutting paper, removing price tags, or cutting up chicken pieces. Mark them somehow as yours. If and when they do get dull you can sharpen them.

For cutting long lengths of rags there is nothing better than a rag cutting machine or a rotary cutter with a guide and self-healing cutting mat. The rag cutting machine has been used for years and is a staple amongst rug hookers, who use it for cutting narrow strips of wool. An adjustable guide lets you cut strips of any width you like. The machine clamps to a table or workbench and works very much like a pasta machine. A metal roller holds the fabric down and pushes it onto a sharp rotating cutting blade; as you turn the handle, the fabric is drawn in and cut to the desired width, and the finished rag strips come out the other end. You simply cut the rags one strip at a time for as many strips as you need or until the fabric is completely cut into strips.

A handheld rotary cutter is another good choice for cutting your rags. It looks much like a small pizza cutter but with an extremely sharp cutting edge that needs to be respected. You will have best results with the rotary cutter if you combine it with a cutting mat and a clear plastic guide. The cutting mat is marked off with ruled measurements on four sides. Simply place the mat on a stable surface and lay your fabric on it. Place the clear plastic guide on top of the fabric at the spot where you want to make the cut and run the rotary cutter along the guide's edge, pressing firmly to go through the fabric. You can fold the fabric to a size that's more manageable and then cut through several layers at once. Blades for the rotary cutter are interchangeable so when a blade gets dull you can simply replace it.

Sewing Machine

In years past, rug makers would sit and sew the cut strips of fabric together by hand. This was a common practice and a good way to pass the time in the evening while listening to the radio. Sometimes people would get together as a social activity and cut and sew rags and catch up with the local gossip. Many hours were spent sewing small fabric strips together by hand. The invention of the sewing machine changed the lives of thousands of households—including those of rag rug weavers. Today's rag rug weaver doesn't need to have the fanciest sewing machine. A machine that will do a few basic functions such as a straight stitch and zigzag stitch is all you need for most aspects of rag rug weaving. If you choose to do a machine-stitched hem, then you will need a heavy-duty sewing machine that can sew through several layers of bulky material.

Washing Machine and Iron

It may seem funny to include a washing machine and an iron on the list of tools for weaving a rag rug, but in fact they are both essential tools. The washing machine is important for preparing the fabric to be woven into the rug—new fabric needs to be washed to remove the finish and preshrink it before it's cut up and incorporated into a rug. You'll need the iron in the finishing process to press a neat hem and to block the rug so it lies flat on the floor. Some people also use an iron in preparing the rags, folding in the cut edges and steam pressing them in place. This makes a neat and clean looking rug but is so time-consuming that many people choose not to press their rags. The iron is such an essential tool that it is worth it to invest in a good-quality professional steam iron that's rather heavy.

Tape Measure

Get a sturdy tape measure that doesn't stretch. You'll want one that measures up to 120 inches; a shorter tape measure will work just fine but for measuring long lengths you will love not having to measure to a certain length and then have to shift the tape and then measure some more.

Pins, T-Pins, and Tapestry Needles

These are just little things, but I promise you will be using all of them all the time. If you don't already have these items among your sewing notions, please go out and buy them.

CHAPTER 2

Materials

The materials used to weave a rag rug can be as diverse as the people who weave them. For their first rag rug, many weavers often choose to weave with traditional materials such as a cotton warp and a weft of cotton rags. Environmentally conscious weavers may choose to only use organic cotton warp threads and never a thread that is petroleum based; for weft they use recycled rags instead of new fabric. Some weavers take the recycling movement to a new level, using grocery bags, newspaper sleeves, washed garbage bags, old nylon stockings, or the legs of panty hose for outdoor mats to wipe your feet on. An acrylic or nylon warp with these unconventional rags makes them easy to wash and nearly indestructible.

When choosing the materials for your rag rug be sure to use well-made and strong warp threads and weft materials that can be washed and will hold up to wear. A well-woven rag rug should last for years—decades, even.

As a collector of old textiles and a self-proclaimed "textologist," I love to look into the worn or torn areas of an old rag rug just to see what materials were used. Sometimes you find treasures in your diagnosis. In one inspection of a nineteenth-century rug I found the warp threads to be the typical cotton warp that you might expect—but the cut rags were from fabrics that you might find in the eighteenth century, fabrics that had been saved for years and eventually found a better use as the filler for this rag carpet.

Let's take a look at the different options of materials for your warp and weft.

Warp Threads

Cotton Thread

Cotton threads are some the most popular and easiest threads to work with, especially if this is your first rag rug. Good-quality cotton rug warp comes in several thread sizes and prepackaged quantities. The most widely used cotton thread is size 8/4 carpet warp, which can be found in dozens of colors. Also available is a line of 8/4 thread that is 50% cotton and 50% polyester. The addition of polyester helps the thread stand up to multiple washings without the fringe disintegrating. Pure cotton doesn't hold up nearly as well in a fringed rug; its short staple length soon unravels and comes apart after multiple washings, leaving you with just the knots at the rug's edge. For weavers who like to use 100% cotton for their warps, a rolled hem is a sensible alternative to a fringe that may not last through lots of washings.

Two more great choices for cotton warp for rag rugs are Seine Twine and Fishgarn. Seine Twine is composed of many strands of plied cotton threads. It is heavy and very, very strong, making it ideal for rug weaving of all kinds. Seine Twine is only available in natural-colored cotton, however. If your plan is to weave a rug that is mostly weft-faced and the warp thread is covered or doesn't play a major role in the design, then Seine Twine may be perfect for you. If your design requires a colored warp, another material may be a

Cotton carpet warp

Heavy mop cotton

better choice. Many good weaving supply stores carry Seine Twine; you can also look for it at your local hardware store (masons use cotton twine for plumb lines to keep brick walls straight, and gardeners will use it for laying out straight rows).

Fishgarn, like Seine Twine, is made up of multiple strands of plied cotton thread. This yarn is imported from Scandinavia and its name means "fish yarn." When you look closely at a piece of Fishgarn, you can see that it resembles the thread used to make fishing nets. Fishgarn comes in a great number of sizes. Some weaving shops carry Fishgarn in a limited number of colors. Though the dyed yarn is noticeably more expensive than natural cotton yarn, it may be worth it to you to have the colored yarn in the rug's design and in the fringe.

Mop cotton is another material that can be used for rug warp. When you hear "mop cotton," mostly likely the stuff on the end of a mop like the kinds school custodians use for cleaning hallways and classroom floors comes to mind. That type of mop cotton is soft spun and is best used in rugs as weft. The mop cotton that I like to use for warp is more tightly spun and is made by plying many strands of finer cotton thread together to create a heavy cotton cord. This type of mop cotton also is available in many colors. It has approximately 400 to 450 yards to the pound, so, as you can see, it is quite heavy and makes a good warp yarn.

Mercerized cotton or Perle cotton is another, often-overlooked option for warp. It has a shiny finish that is the effect of an alkali solution that polishes the thread. Perle cotton is readily available in heavier-weight threads such as 3/2 and 5/2 cotton and is dyed to dozens of beautiful colors. When a design such as rep weave calls for a rug to be warp-faced or warp emphasized, I will often turn to Perle cotton for my warp. Perle cotton is very strong and can easily take the abrasion that's put on the threads in weaving warp-faced rugs and runners. Its shiny, almost silklike appearance gives a rag rug a more formal appearance. Perle cotton would also be an excellent choice for rag placemats and table runners.

Linen Thread

Linen thread is very strong and hard wearing, and an excellent choice for rag rugs. Because linen is also very dense, a rug woven with a linen warp (or for that matter with a linen warp and linen rag weft) will lie flat on the floor and will shift around less than rugs made with less-dense materials. One important characteristic of linen thread to keep in mind is it has little to no elasticity; it doesn't give or spring back into position if knocked with your shuttle. Because of this, you need to make sure your warp threads are evenly tensioned when working with linen. This is more easily achieved when weaving on a floor loom, especially a deep (long from the front to the back) countermarch or counterbalance loom. Rug linen is available in its natural color of gray-brown, which makes it a nice neutral base for any color of rags that you wish to weave into it. The standard sizes for rug linen are 8/2, 8/3, 8/4, and 8/5. The second number refers to the number of plies to the thread so the larger this number is the thicker the thread. The first number indicates the size of the individual thread. This numbering system is standard in the textile industry and is used to identify many weaving threads. Treat yourself to a linen warp sometime and compare for yourself the differences between linen and cotton warp.

Seine Twine and linen rug warp

Wool Yarn
Rag rug weavers rarely use wool for rug warp. Somehow this fiber just gets overlooked. But it doesn't need to be! I personally love to combine wool rags with a wool warp that is well spun and plied. Over time and with use, the wool warp threads bind with the woolen rags in a process known as felting. Look for a 3- or 4-ply wool that is tightly spun without a lot of elasticity. You need a yarn that is rough or even hairy. Never use a knitting yarn. Knitting yarns are made from varieties of sheep that provide soft wool and the yarns are spun with a gentle twist, giving the yarn some stretch when you pull on it. Wool rug warp can be found in a variety of colors as well as the natural colors of sheep wool; you can also dye the natural wool, even blacks, grays, and browns, which will give you deep, rich colors, adding lots of beauty and interest to your rugs. Imagine weaving strips of heather wool fabric into a gray tweed warp. Fantastic!

Tightly spun wool warp

Synthetic Yarn
I have to admit that I don't associate the old timey charm of a rag rug with synthetic materials. But why not? These yarns were developed to make our lives more comfortable and washing and ironing less labor intensive. Acrylic, nylon, and polyester yarns and threads can be used as warp yarns, with the exception of those acrylic yarns that are meant to be knitting yarns. Ask your weaving store owner if they carry an acrylic rug warp about the size of 8/4 cotton. This will be a sturdy thread that can take the stress of weaving and beating the rags back into the web. As mentioned earlier, you can buy polyester-cotton-blend 8/4 carpet warp, which comes in a variety of colors. The advantage of using synthetics for your warp is in the finishing of the rug. A fringe made from synthetic fibers will hold up well to wear and washing.

Weft Fabrics

When thinking about the rags for your rug, you have a lot of choices. You can recycle fabric by cutting up unwanted clothing, sheets, and blankets just as the weavers did in the past. Or you can buy new fabric for options that go far beyond what you can get from repurposing old and unwanted clothes. When you go into a large fabric store it is sometimes overwhelming. There are so many types of fabric to choose from, and the selection of colors is vast. Don't be afraid to ask for help (although once you've read this chapter you may have more insight into which fabrics would be best for a rag rug than many fabric store employees).

Look around the store and start by eliminating the fabrics you don't want. You will quickly get a feel for it. Burlap, bridal veiling with hand-sewn pearls, leatherette and upholstery fabrics are not first on my list either. Although you could use any of these materials for weaving a rag rug it's unlikely that you would want to cut them into strips and weave them into a warp. But don't dismiss wild and crazy prints. What you might find hideous just may turn out to be a wonderful choice when crunched down into a rug. I once found a printed cotton fabric showing a map of the world with each country in a different color. *Who would want this and how would you use it?* I thought. But the price was perfect at two dollars a yard, and I had a coupon that I could use. To my surprise, the material wove up into a spectacular rag rug. The prints with cartoon super heroes and holiday themes are also good.

Even before you think of color or design, you need to think about what type of fabric you want to use—cotton, linen, wool, or something else. Let's break this down to some of the best fabric options to try for rag rugs.

Cotton and Cotton Blends
Solid-color cottons and cotton prints are always good. With solid-color fabric both sides of the fabric are fully saturated with the color, and you don't have to worry about one side of the fabric being lighter than the other. With cotton prints the pattern is pressed onto the fabric and the dye bleeds through to the back, leaving a fainter version of what the front of the fabric looks like. Try to look for prints with good color saturation on the reverse side so you don't feel the need to fold the cut strips to hide the lighter side of the fabric. If the fabric you're weaving with is much lighter on the reverse side and you make no attempt to hide the lighter side, the rag strip will twist and both sides will appear within the same row of

■ HOW MUCH FABRIC DO I NEED FOR A RAG RUG?

Calculating the amount of warp you need is really quite straightforward. You determine the sett, or number of ends per inch (EPI), that corresponds to the type of warp you are using, then multiply that by the width and length you intend to make the rug. We'll revisit these calculations in greater detail in chapter 14.

Calculating the amount of weft fabric you will be using is another story. There is no easy formula, and it can be difficult to figure out how much of a particular fabric you need to make a rug.

I once asked an older individual who was not a weaver but remembered preparing rags for the weaver in their community how much fabric they gave the weaver to make a rug. Their answer was "several feed bags." This individual, like so many people, prepared the weft by cutting up old pieces of clothing and sewing the short lengths together. Then they would wind them into balls to take to the weaver for their rag rugs. This was an interesting insight into the preparation of rags for weaving rugs in the early twentieth century but it was of no help to me if I wanted to go to the store and buy fabric for a new rug by the yard.

Books on the weaving of rag rugs always give the same answer: To weave a rag rug approximately 3 feet by 5 feet, you need about 5 to 6 pounds of rags. This was an answer but still not a very useful one. I could just image myself going into a national fabric chain store with a baby scale under my arm, plopping it on the counter and then asking the salesperson to just keep unwinding the bolt until we reached 6 pounds. Yeah, right!

I decided to do a little experimenting. I bought one yard each of several different fabrics, cut them into 1½ inch wide strips, and then wove them into a warp of 8/4 cotton carpet warp set at 12 ends per inch, 12 inches wide in the reed. This way, I could see exactly how much coverage I could get from my one yard of each of the fabrics. At last, I would get a definitive answer to how much fabric it would take to weave a square foot of a rag rug!

The answer is that there is no definitive answer. On average, one yard of apparel-weight cotton fabric or quilters' cotton will yield about one square foot of a rag rug (most times it took a little less than a yard of fabric to weave a square foot, so buying a full yard of fabric was like having insurance). But the story changes with heavier fabrics like denim, corduroy, and coat-weight wool. When I wove these fabrics I cut the strips to a width of 1 inch because the fabrics were so much heavier and thicker. These samples often wove to 16 to 18 inches. So what I found was that heavier-weight fabrics require much less yardage to cover a square foot.

So use my discoveries as a preliminary guide, but when in doubt, always weave a sample using a yard of the fabric that you are planning to use. It isn't always fun to weave samples, and sometimes it feels like a waste of time and materials, but is so important to get the infortmation we need. There is so much variation between different rugs. For instance, a rag rug that is weft dominant will require a lot more rags because of the way the weft slides down tightly on top of the last weft pick; a rag rug that is warp dominant will require less fabric because there is more resistance and the beater cannot beat the weft in as tightly.

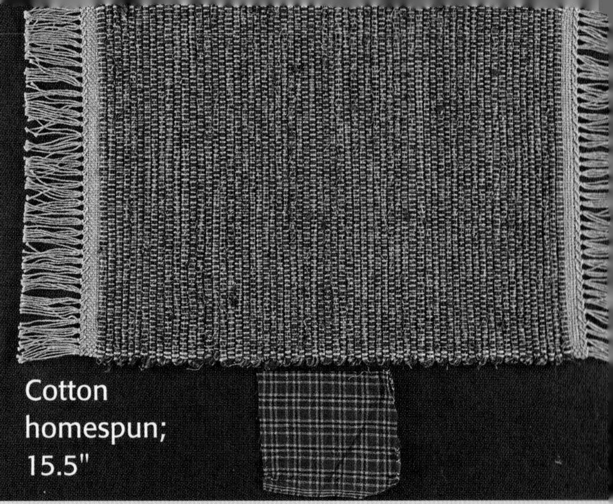

Cotton homespun; 15.5"

Suit-weight 100% wool; 42"

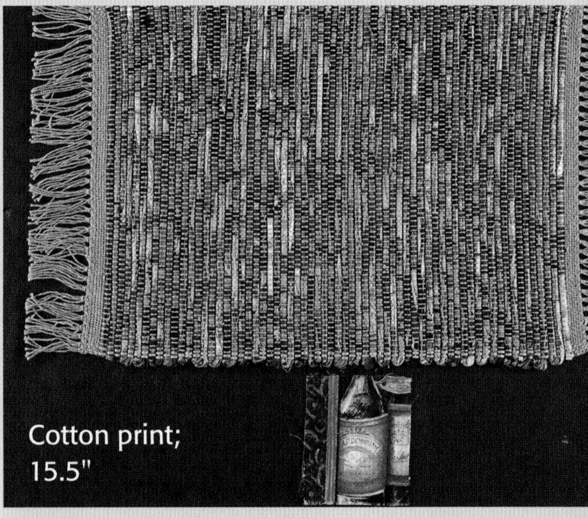

Cotton print; 15.5"

Cotton print; 14"

Shirt-weight 100% linen; 20"

Small-wale corduroy; 18"

Cotton print; 14.5"

100% cotton quilting fabric; 13.5"

Cotton denim; 25"

100% cotton quilting fabric; 16.5"

Cotton flannel; 28"

Cotton batik; 14"

the woven rug. The result is a mottled effect—which can be quite beautiful, if that's the look you're going for.

There are some patterned cottons that are the same on both sides. Batiks usually have colorful and bold patterns and look the same on both sides. They are more expensive than printed cottons but well worth the extra cost when you see how easy they are to weave. Gingham and plaid patterned fabrics are woven with different colors of thread in the warp and weft; the "homespun" aisle will have old timey and country-style patterns woven from dyed threads. These types of fabric will look the same, or similar, on both sides.

Also consider cotton fabrics in other textures. Flannels are wonderful to use as rags and the finished rug will feel delightful under your feet. The soft luxurious feel of flannel makes these rag rugs the perfect choice to put beside your bed and to step onto first thing in the morning. Both denim and corduroy hold up to lots of wear. Rugs woven from denim and corduroy can be placed in high-traffic areas where they are stepped upon regularly and pick up a lot of dirt. Their durability makes them also easy to wash and vacuum. Rag rugs woven from the legs of denim jeans are practically beautiful because of the different degrees of wear on the fabric. There may be dozens of shades of indigo blue in just one rug woven from old worn jeans. When you spiral cut the legs of a pair of blue jeans, the side seams add textural interest and a rustic look to the rug.

Cotton Knits

Knitted cotton fabrics can also be used in rag rugs—and, of course, they come with their own advantages and challenges. A knitted material will stretch more than a woven fabric so working with knits presents some challenges. To prevent excessive draw-in as you weave your rug, pull hard on the rag strip and stretch it as you wind the shuttle. By stretching the fabric out of shape you help to guarantee that it won't draw back to its original form. Look to see how much thinner the rag is now that you pulled on it. To keep with tradition of using a thicker weft to weave a heavy rug you might want to cut the knit fabric twice as wide as you would a woven fabric strip.

A rag rug is a marvelous way to use up a collection of old T-shirts. When you think about the color of the shirt itself and then add the printed graphics on top you can't help but have a handsome strip of rag. You can mix lots of colors from dozens of different tee shirts or go with a theme. Try using the old tee shirts collected from just one source such as your child's soccer team. This way you will get a lot of material that's already prewashed and all in the same color theme.

When weaving a rug with knits keep to only knit fabric. Do not mix knits with woven strips. By mixing the two you risk ending up with a rug that may buckle and not lay flat on the floor. You may think that all that preshrinking of the fabric from washing and all the pulling and stretching would stabilize the rag strips. Well, it might work and you might get lucky—but personally, I don't take the risk. Remember to weave "wovens with wovens and knits with knits. Never mix them together or they will give you fits."

Linen Fabric

Linen is a dense, heavy fabric; rugs woven from it are heavy, lie flat on the floor, and don't shift around as easily as rugs from other materials. It is expensive, however, requiring you to get creative. Look for sales or use those discount coupons from national chain stores and buy the whole bolt. I like using suit-weight linen fabric for my rag rugs, but finding it in colors has proved to be quite a challenge. I will buy an entire bolt of natural-color linen and then dye the fabric myself; the easiest way to do this is to dye the fabric and then cut the rag strips. (Please, never the other way round. You will end up with a ball of tangled rag strips.) Because of the high cost of linen and its limited selections in stores, you might want to try asking your friends and relatives if they have any old linen tablecloths that they don't want anymore. Because of our relaxed habits of entertaining these days, few people are using linen table cloths and napkins. You may be surprised at how many of your friends are storing old wedding presents in their attics and are only too happy to give you sets of never-used tablecloths. Just please promise me you will never cut up antique hand-woven linens. Those beautiful old handspun and hand-woven linens with indigo blue or brown checks should be given respect and placed into the hands of people who will truly love them. Send them to me! Another good source for linen material is used clothing stores such as Salvation Army and Goodwill. Sometimes people will donate linen shirts, skirts, and dresses because they don't want to be bothered with ironing them. Goody for you though. It's a cheap way to acquire a collection of linen rags.

Wool and Wool Blends

Weaving with wool or any protein-based fiber is pure joy. Protein-based fiber refers to any fiber that originated from an animal. Other fabrics that are protein based include mohair, camel hair, alpaca, and silk. All of these fabrics are luxury fabrics and expensive to buy as on-the-bolt material, so if you want to use wool you'll likely want to start gathering secondhand wool fabric. Putting together a collection of wool rags from old clothing takes some time. Start by looking at thrift stores, yard sales, church sales, and community outreach shops for jackets, coats, skirts, and blankets that you can take apart and cut into rag strips. The strips will be short in length but this gives you the opportunity to mix colors. Try placing dark colors next to lighter colors and warm colors alternating with cool colors for a pleasing hit-and-miss look to your rug. Wool and protein based fabrics (even if they contain a small percentage of nylon or other synthetic) are some of the easiest to dye. Even darker fabrics such as charcoal and dark browns can be overdyed to get deep, rich colors; these types of colors are more challenging to achieve when starting with natural white. If you buy new fabric to cut into rag strips look for medium to heavy suit-weight or coat-weight fabric. These weave into a plush-feeling rug. Your feet will thank you for caring. Start by looking at your local fabric stores and don't forget to watch for those discount coupons offered by some of the chains. I have used online stores as well and found them to be wonderful for their prices, shipping costs, and delivery times.

Other Materials

There are some very nice synthetic fabrics on the market that make wonderful rags. Polar fleece, because of its remarkable softness and the way it washes so easily, is a good choice for rag rug strips. It comes in lots of pretty colors and is reasonably priced. You could buy enough for a bedspread plus enough to weave into matching rugs for the sides of the bed.

I personally steer clear of rayons and nylons because of their slippery nature. When you weave a rag rug with rayon or nylon the rug tends to slide around on the floor and becomes a hazard to walk on. A box full of satin binding may at first seem like a gift—already precut and ready to weave. But the resulting rug will be slick and may cause you to fall if you don't put a skid-proof mat under the rug.

The "loopers" that are made from sock tops and sold for making pot holders are also a nice alternative to weaving with fabric strips. By interlocking the loopers end to end you can make a long continuous length of weft material.

For a rag rug that needs to be really hard wearing and take a lot of washings, try using nylon stockings, pantyhose, and tights. These come in lots of shades of natural skin tones as well as colors such as green, blue, purple, red, and white. They are made of nylon, so they would be slippery and dangerous on a tile floor, but for a rug to put outside on a wooden deck, they would be just fine.

You can even try weaving with recycled plastic bags from the grocery store. Spiral-cut the bags into long strips and weave away! This type of rug is best cleaned by hosing it off and leaving it outside to dry.

These are just a few suggestions of the materials you can try—there are many possibilities and people are always thinking of new ones. Once I was attending a craft show in Washington, DC, and came across a weaver with the most beautiful rag rugs. The rugs had a textured appearance and soft colors that were very appealing. When I explained that I was a weaver also and was wondering about her weft materials, the weaver generously divulged her secret: She uses old wool sweaters that she picks up at yard sales and consignment stores and from friends and relatives that are cleaning out their winter clothes. She washes and dries them in the dryer until they are half their original size; with the sweaters felted and shrunk up tightly she can cut them into strips and weave with them just the way they are. They are so tightly felted that the strips simply can't unravel.

You don't need to spend a lot of money on your first rag rug endeavor. Remember, the first rag rugs were woven by frugal people who made their own rugs and carpeting from old, worn-out clothing. Don't overthink it—just jump in and weave a rug!

CHAPTER 3

Preparing the Rags

Now that you've selected your fabric—whether it's a new off-bolt cotton print, a bag of old wool skirts from a thrift store, or a collection of linen tablecloths donated by friends—and calculated how much you'll need, it's time to prepare it for being woven into the rug.

Washing the Fabric

If you're using new fabric, the first step is to wash it to remove the finish that's placed on it at the mill. (Just walk into a fabric store and take a deep breath. You can *smell* the finish!) Washing and drying the fabric also makes cutting and tearing the fabric much easier and preshrinks the fabric so you don't experience as much shrinkage with the first washing of the rug. Beating is easier as well with prewashed rags. I either line dry the fabric or put it into the dryer but I do not use fabric softener or dryer sheets, which just put another layer of chemicals on the surface of the fabric.

If you are planning on weaving a wool rag rug it's advisable to felt the fabric. Take the length of new fabric (or recycled wool from clothing) and wash it on a regular cycle with hot water and a cold rinse to tighten it up and shrink it. Today high-efficiency washing machines with front end loading to conserve water usage are popular; although these machines do a marvelous job with the family clothes they tend not to be the best for felting wool. If you are going to work with wool rags you might want to use a top loader (if you or a friend has one—or go to a laundromat). These machines work great for felting wool rags.

Now for a word of caution from your author: Wash your rags *before* you cut them! Without thinking, I once placed a large amount of precut rag strips, each several yards long, into the washer to remove the finish. As the rag strips washed they entangled themselves around the agitator. This is a mess that I hope you never have to deal with. If you do come across some precut rags (such factory ends) and want to wash them, place them in a laundry bag that closes at on end. You will be so glad you did.

Preparing Purchased Fabric

Now it's time to cut or tear the strips. This is a dusty job, do it in a large room with lots of space or even outside. If you are sensitive to this sort of work, you should wear a dust mask to protect your lungs.

I like tearing my fabric strips. It's quick and easy, though it does have some drawbacks. You often end up with a frayed edge and lots of loose threads to deal with. I don't mind this at all—actually, I like the look. After all, it is a rag rug! The straggling loose threads can be pulled off as you wind the strips of fabric onto the shuttle.

Tear the strips with the length of the fabric to get the longest fabric strips you can. Start by making cuts about 4 to 5 inches deep along one cut end of your fabric at the width that you want your strips to be (about 1½ inch for quilting cotton, shirt-weight fabric, and flannel; 1 inch for denim and wool). I make a cardboard template to help maintain even

Tearing strips with a friend

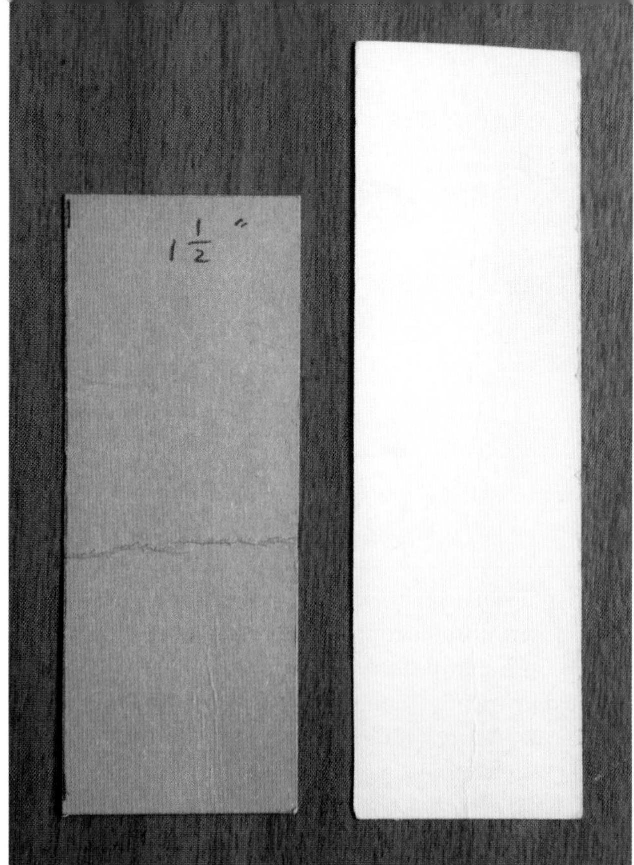

Templates

widths. You can also just measure it out with a tape measure or yardstick.

Then simply grab ahold of the fabric strip that your deep cut started and tear down the length of your fabric.

If you precut all the deep cuts into the fabric you can recruit a friend to help and you two will have the time of your lives. Start by holding onto the first strip and let your friend grab the next strip. You then take the next strip and your friend the next. Keep alternating the strips between you two and then start pulling against each other in opposite directions. It's a lot like having a tug of war. Giggles and laughter are often experienced by the participants.

Not all fabrics will tear easily. Wool, linen, and twill weaves are a challenge and may not tear at all. You will then need to resort to a pair of scissors or rug cutter.

To cut your fabric you need obviously a very sharp pair of scissors or a cutter. Cut along the length of the fabric to your desired width. If you get a little off in your measurement, it is not the end of the world. It will all level out in the weaving.

I like using a rotary cutter with a cutting mat and guide to cut my strips. If your fabric is not too long—say, just a few yards long—you can fold it into several layers and lay the fabric onto the mat. Then place the clear Lucite guide on top of the fabric and, using your rotary cutter, slice through all the layers at once, creating a nice long strip of fabric.

I have also used a fabric cutting machine that is often used to cut wool fabric for hooked rugs. This cutter attaches to a work table and has a guide that you can adjust to the width of the strips you want. Place the fabric on the tray of the cutter, with the edge along the guide. Turn the handle to draw the fabric into the cutter; the resulting cut strip comes out the other end. It's somewhat like a pasta machine, though it only does one strip at a time.

After the fabric strips are cut or torn I like to taper the ends by making a diagonal cut that's about 4 to 5 inches long on each end. This way, as you are weaving and your strip comes to the end you can easily overlap the new strip over the old one and beat it down into place without any sign of a join (unless the new strip is a different color).

If you are working with shorter lengths of fabric, say 2 yards or less, you might want to try a zigzag cutting method. Lay your fabric out on a table. Start cutting your first strip with a pair of scissors along the edge of the fabric, stopping about 2 inches from the end. *Do not cut all the way through the end.* Move to the other side of the fabric and start making the next cut, for a strip approximately the same width as the first. Again, stop about 2 inches from the end.

Continue this way until you have worked all across the piece of fabric. The strips will have a zigzag appearance and an awkward look at the ends where you didn't cut all the way through. To ease the turn and help to straighten out the strip, simply make tapered cuts at the corners. This will reduce the bulk and help to straighten the fabric.

Preparing Recycled Fabric

Some people like the idea of recycling old clothes to make rag rugs. If you start cutting apart an old shirt or coat, you will quickly see that the strips produced are short and are going to require sewing together to get a strip long enough to wind onto a shuttle.

Joining shorter lengths of fabric may seem to be a nuisance but the overall effect in the woven rug is beautiful. We call these rugs "hit-or-miss" rugs. They had their heyday in the early years of weaving rag rugs because this was the most common way of preparing the rag strips. Back then, rag rug makers were in the mindset of using what they had and would never have gone out and bought new fabric to cut into rags. Though it's common to buy new material for a rag rug today, the traditional hit-or-miss style is still a great way to make a unique and beautiful rug.

If you are going to sew short lengths of rag together there are two easy ways to do this. For one option, start by overlapping two ends of your strips for about an inch. Then fold them lengthwise. This is a great time to be sure that the wrong side of fabric is turned inside and the pretty side is toward the outside. Using a needle and thread, sew back and forth through the layers to secure them.

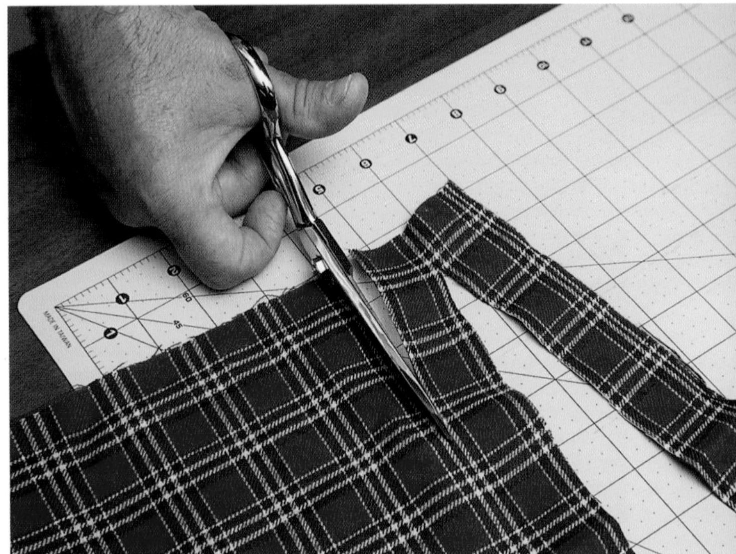

Cutting strips using the zigzag method

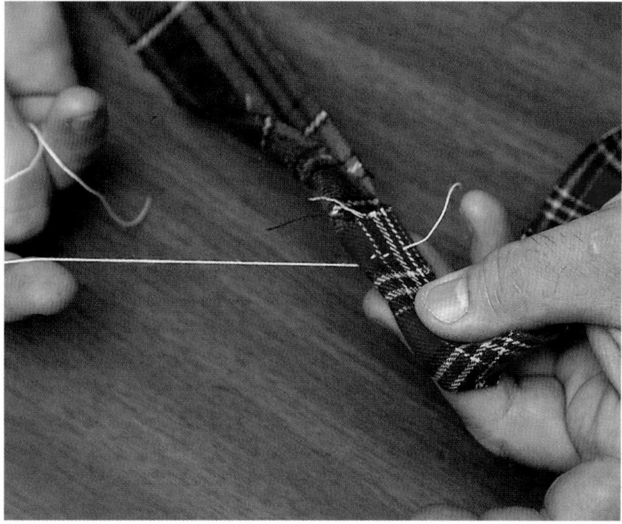

Another way to secure the ends is to overlap the ends as before for about an inch and then sew them on a diagonal. This can be done by hand or with a sewing machine. To reduce the bulk you can cut and remove the free ends.

Shorter lengths can also be joined together without sewing by cutting small slits (about an inch long) on either end of the fabric strip, creating a small hole on each end. Fold the end of the strip back onto itself for about 1 inch, then cut into the fold for about ½ inch, being careful that you don't cut all the way to the end of the strip. You'll see a hole at the end of your strip when you unfold it.

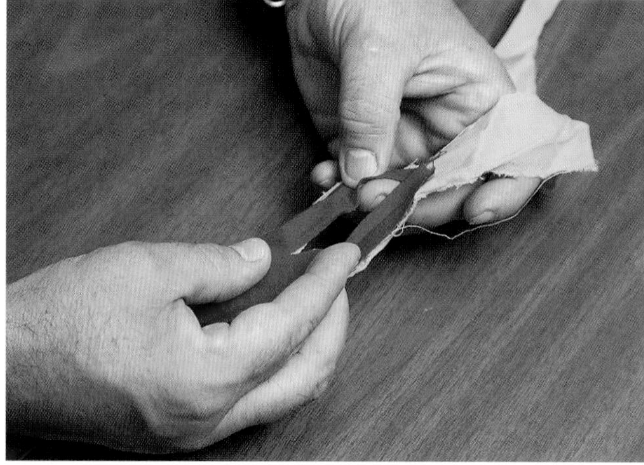

When you've cut holes in both ends of several strips, you are ready to start joining them together. Start by laying the first piece to your left. Now lay the second strip, coming in from the right, on top of the first strip. Match up the holes or slits.

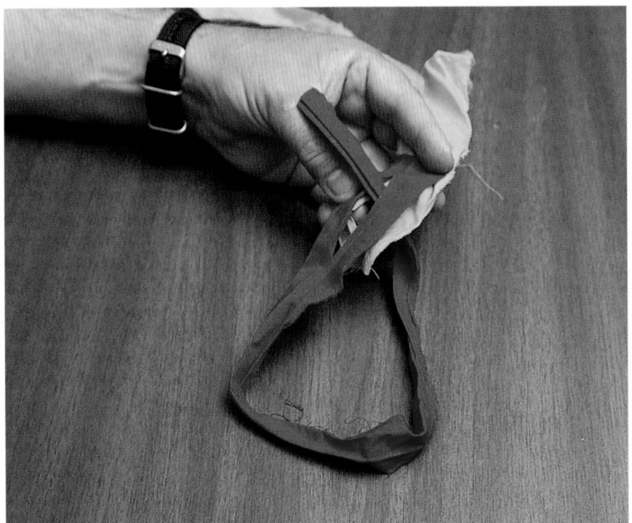

Hold the join with your left hand and with your right hand bring the other end of the right strip underneath the hole and bring this end up through the hole.

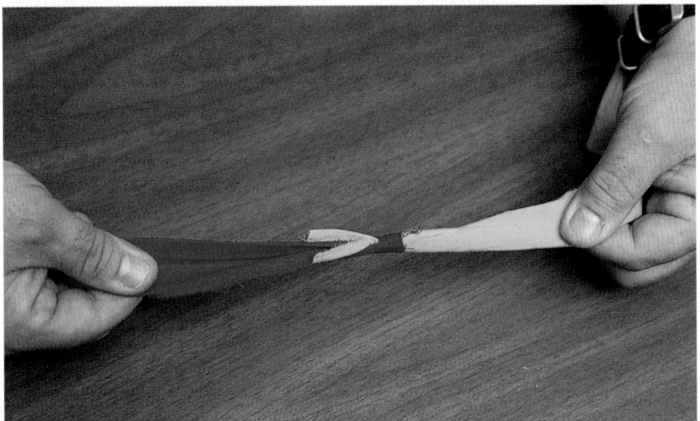

Gently pull on the two strips of fabric to interlock them.

This will make a small bump, but the bumps will add a pleasing texture to the surface of your rug. They can also cause difficulty in beating the strip down into the rug, and create buckles that prevent your rug from lying flat on the floor. To avoid this, be sure that the warp is set wider in the reed. A wider setting such as 6 or 8 ends per inch will produce a larger space for the seam bumps to poke through and allow the rug to lie flat. If you try weaving these strips into a rug warp that has a closer sett of 12 to 24 ends per inch, you will definitely experience buckling because the warp threads will have to ride on top of the seam bumps instead of passing to the right or left.

It is possible to bypass the sewing with some creative cutting. With a pair of slacks or old blue jeans, you can get long strips by making spiral cuts up the legs of the pants. Start by cutting the legs off the pants up near the crotch, below the back pockets. Now begin to cut around and around the leg on a very slight angle to keep a continuous cut going—the way they cut a spiral ham. You can start at the top or bottom of the leg; it doesn't matter which.

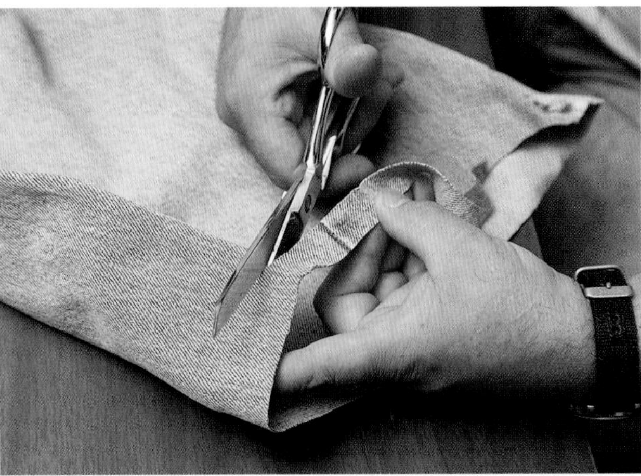

Cut straight through the bulky part of the vertical seam. This may seem very odd but you are doing fine. These lumps and bumps will add texture to the surface of your rug. Just be sure that your warp is set wide enough in the reed to allow the bumps to surface, as I described before with the interlocked short strips.

■ RIGHT SIDE/WRONG SIDE

One final thing to check before you can start weaving with your rags is whether there is a similar amount of color on both sides of the fabric. As I mentioned in the previous chapter, batik fabrics are wonderful because they look the same on both sides; many other fabrics are printed and have an obvious good side and not-so-good side. This may not bother you at all because the mix of the two sides can create an attractive look. If the wrong side of the fabric shows up only occasionally, however, it looks like a mistake.

To get a crisp look without any wrong-side mishaps, it is worth the time to fold the fabric in thirds and iron the strips. It takes a little of your time but is truly worth the effort. Starting at one end of a rag strip, fold about a third of the fabric in on itself lengthwise and give a light pressing for about a foot or less. Then fold the other edge in and press it to match. It is a little awkward a first but you will soon develop a system for doing it quickly. Your finished woven rug will look much neater without the inside of the print showing up on the surface of the rug.

Preparing Knit Fabric

Many of us remember making woven pot holders from "loopers" on small square looms in our childhoods. These "loopers" were waste material from factories that made socks—and they are still available today. You can use these sock tops to make rugs but it is going to take a lot of them to make one rug. Interconnect the loops with each other to make a long strip that can be wound onto a rug shuttle. Because the sock tops are made from a knitted fabric, they are very stretchy. I usually try to avoid knit fabric for this reason; the stretchy fabric makes the rugs width draw in severely, making it difficult to know just how wide the finished rug will be. You can help to avoid this by pulling on the loops and stretching them out of shape.

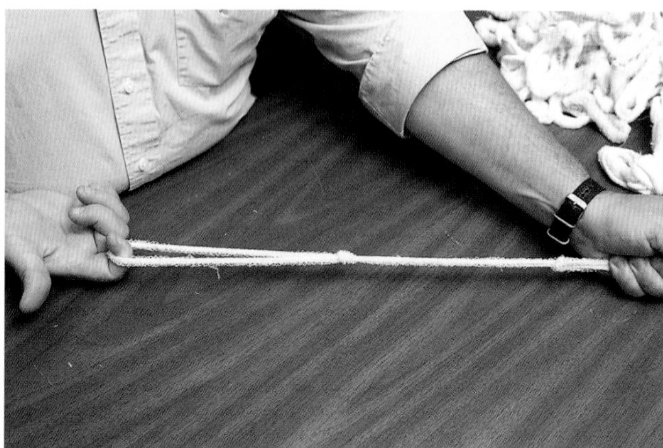

You can also make your own giant loopers from old T-shirts. Start by laying the T-shirt onto a flat work table and straighten it out so it lies flat. With scissors or a rotary cutter and cutting mat, remove the waistband. Now move up approximately ½" and cut all the way across the two layers of the shirt to make your first looper.

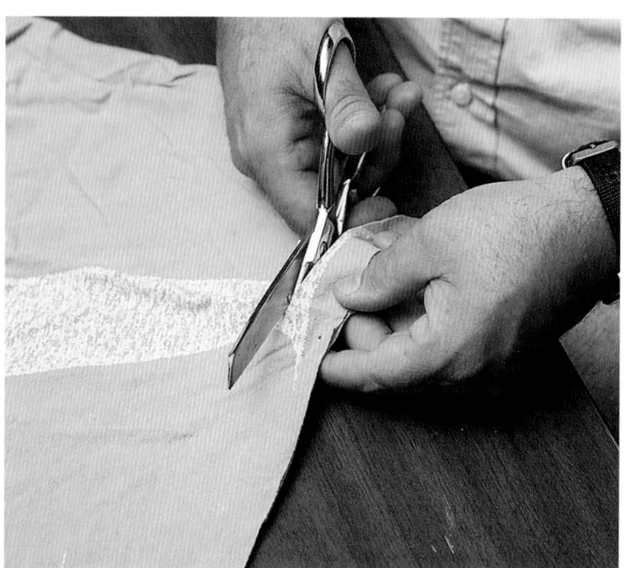

The side seams remain joined, of course, creating a large loop. Because you have ½" of fabric on each side of the loop, you have now the equivalent of 1" total fabric in your loop. Take a moment to admire your loop. Ta-Da! Now how great is that I ask you?

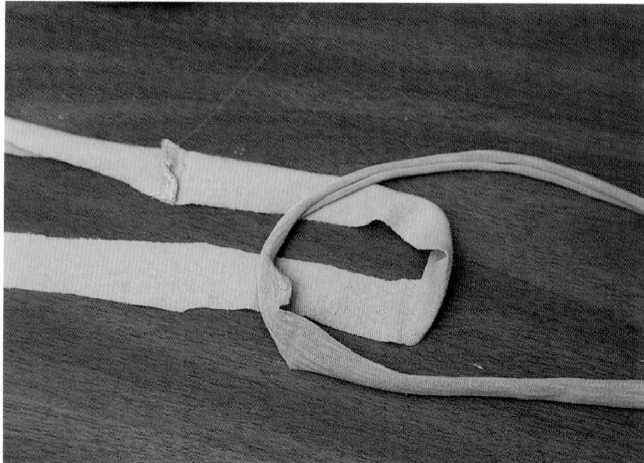

Sock top loopers and T-shirt loopers are joined together the same way. Start by placing a looper to the right of you. Bring a second looper in from the left side and overlap the two loopers so that the edge of the looper on the right is lying on top of the left looper.

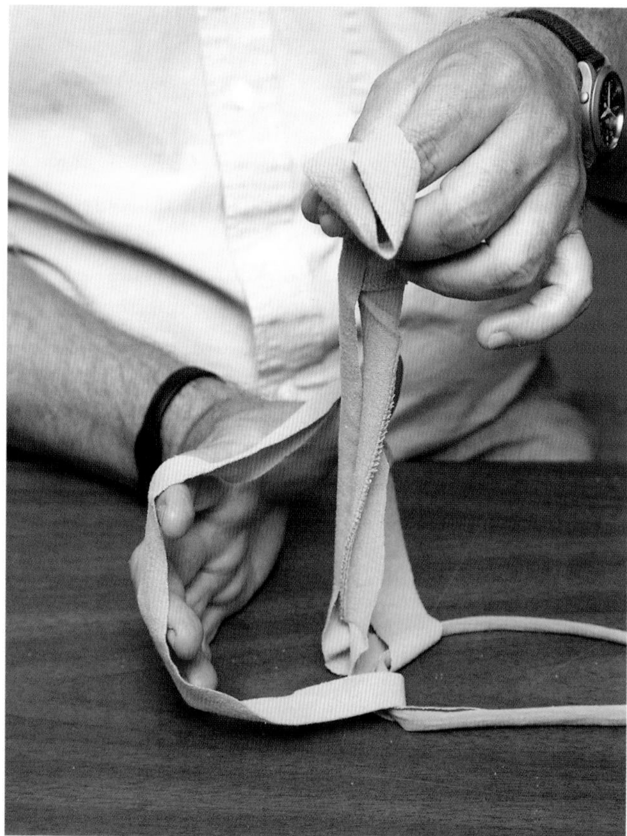

Now bring the far end of the left looper toward the overlap and loop it up through itself.

Pull the loopers away from each other to tighten the knot.

The pulling will also stretch the knitted fabric and make it more stable. When you pull the loopers the raw and cut edges curl inward, making the looper more tubular and round; this is because it is knitted fabric.

If you have a collection of different shirts of all sizes and colors you will of course have loopers of all lengths and colors. Mix them up and loop them together to weave fabulous-looking rag rugs. Try making a theme rug by using only T-shirts donated from the players on your child's soccer team. Any of the printed graphics on the shirt will only add colorful interest to the rug's surface. What a nice thank-you gift for the coach!

I have friends who make plastic grocery bag loopers and weave them into durable entryway rugs. These are so easy to wash—or just hose them off and hang them to dry on the line or porch railing.

Close-up of an unbalanced weave

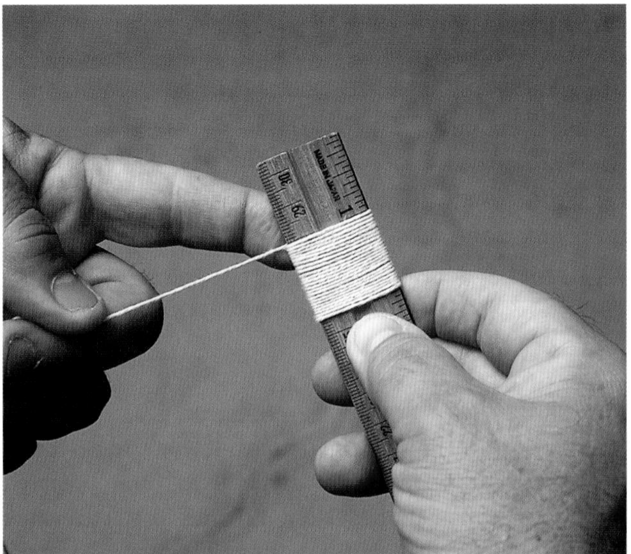

Finding the EPI

These last few examples are clearly unbalanced. Most woven rag rugs fall into an area that is a little unclear, with a setting of 12 to 16 EPI. You could weave with 8/4 cotton thread for both warp and weft at this setting and get a perfectly lovely (balanced) cotton fabric. But in a rag rug the weft material is strips of fabric that are proportionately much larger and heavier, making it an unbalanced weave; with the warp set at 12 to 16 EPI, the weft picks are 4 or 5.

Now to calculate the EPI for your rug. Start by taking a ruler and the thread you intend to use as your warp. In this case we are using 8/4 cotton carpet warp. Wrap the carpet warp firmly around the ruler, placing the threads side by side. If you see the ruler showing through the wraps, you are not getting the threads as close as they need to be—you are trying to calculate the warp as it will be on the loom, under tension. Wrap for 1 inch, then count the threads; 8/4 cotton will have 24 wraps in a 1-inch space on the ruler, but with a different thread you may get a different figure. Now divide this number in half for plain weave or tabby, or by-two thirds for twill. This is the standard for calculating all yarns and threads. In our example, 24 divided by 2 for tabby will give you a setting of 12 EPI. For twill, divide 24 by two-thirds to get 16 EPI.

■ DRAW-IN

This is the perfect time to talk about draw-in. Draw-in is the narrowing of your rug that happens as you weave. Some rag rugs draw in more than others. Weft-face twill may draw in as much as 10 to 15 percent, while a warp-face rug will not draw in at all and might actually measure slightly wider than what it was set in the reed because of the density of the warp. On average, there is very little draw-in with a conventional rag rug with a sett of 12 to 16 EPI and woven with rags 1 to 1½" wide. If you think that you might experience some draw-in in your rug, be sure to add a little extra to the width in the reed to compensate.

Now let's calculate the total number of ends or warp threads. Simply multiply the EPI by the width in the reed. For a rug woven as tabby and measuring 25 inches wide in the reed, we get 12 EPI times 25, or 300 total ends or threads. For a twill structure, take 16 EPI times 25, for a total of 400 total ends or threads.

Next, you need to calculate the warp length. First, think about how long you want the finished rug to be. Then add 20 percent more to that number for take-up (extra length needed to account for the warp threads going over and under the weft threads instead of straight up the loom). There is quite a lot of take-up when weaving rag rugs because the weft materials are so thick and heavy. When you are weaving conventional fabric, you only need to add 10 percent. If you are planning on weaving with an extremely heavy weft material add an additional 25 to 30 percent (i.e., 45 to 50 percent total). This is like having insurance to cover you for the unexpected, especially if you haven't woven a sample first. Some individuals like to weave a sample and calculate exactly what the take up will be; I tend to add extra right from the beginning and weave by the seat of my pants, knowing that I have that insurance built in. Next, think about how you are going to finish the rug. Will there be fringe or will you weave a hem? If you are planning on weaving a hem, allow about

3 inches on each end for the woven area of hem; if you are planning on a fringe, then allow about 6 inches extra on each end. Add the finished length, the take-up, and the hem or fringe allowance to get the length you need to weave one rug. If you are planning on weaving several rugs on the same warp, then multiply this number by the number of rugs you are planning on weaving. *You're not done yet!* The final factor to add in is what is known as loom waste. This is the area of the warp that is used to tie onto the apron rods, front and back, and also the unwoven area from the last weft row of your weaving that continues back and through the reed and harness frames to where you tied onto the back apron rod. You should usually add between 30 and 36 inches for loom waste, depending on your loom. Add this figure in to your total, and you have the final length for each strand of warp.

Now that you have calculated the warp length, it is time to measure out the warp on either a warping board or a warping mill.

The method I use for warping my loom is known as warping front to back. In this method, you place the measured warp into the reed first and then go to the back of the loom and thread the heddles, tie the warp to the apron rod, wind it onto the warp beam, and finally go the front to tie the warp onto the front apron rod and adjust the tension. Let's break this process down into smaller, easy-to-follow steps.

Warping mill

Warping board

Winding the Warp

You can wind the warp either on a warping board or on a warping mill. They have exactly the same function: to measure each thread in the warp to the same length. Often, you can wind the entire warp for your rug all at one time. This is because the pegs on the warping board and mill are long and can accommodate the many passes you need to make to measure out the total number of warp threads. Warping boards are inexpensive in comparison to warping mills. If you are handy, you can even make your own warping board. In our example here, I'll show you how to wind the warp using a warping board.

1. Start by making a guide thread in a contrasting color. Measure it to the same length as your desired warp length, then add a few inches for tying it onto the pegs of the board. This guide thread will outline the path that you are going to take with the actual warp. It is only a guide and not part of the warp.

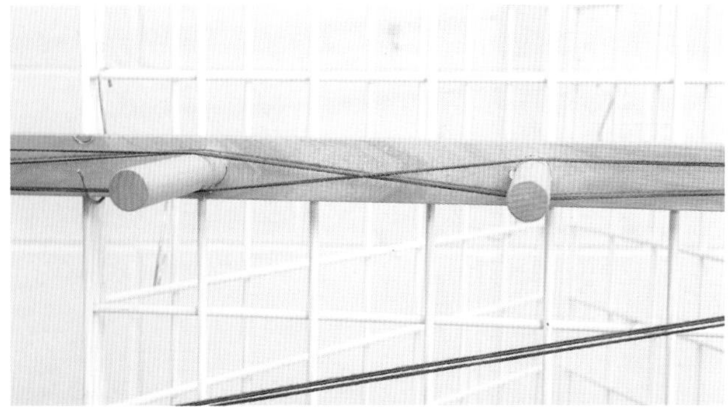

2. Look at the warping board and locate the area where there are three pegs placed rather close together (on the upper left on the warping board shown here). This is the spot where you are going to be winding the warp in a figure eight, and it is referred to as "the cross." The cross helps you keep the threads in a chronological order. This helps you to remember the thread order when placing them in the reed later on.

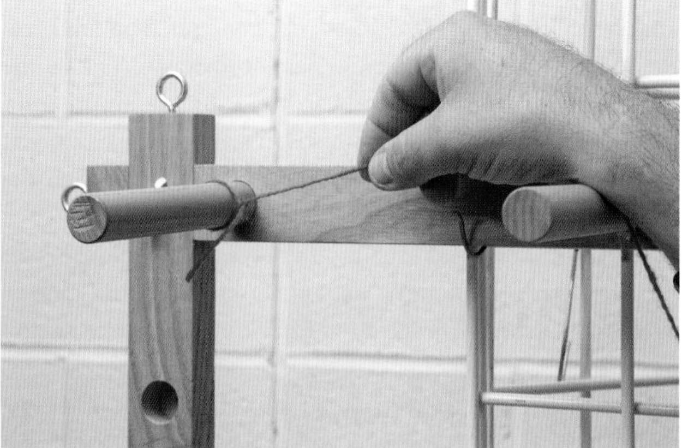

3. Start by tying the guide thread onto the first peg at the beginning of the warping board near the cross.

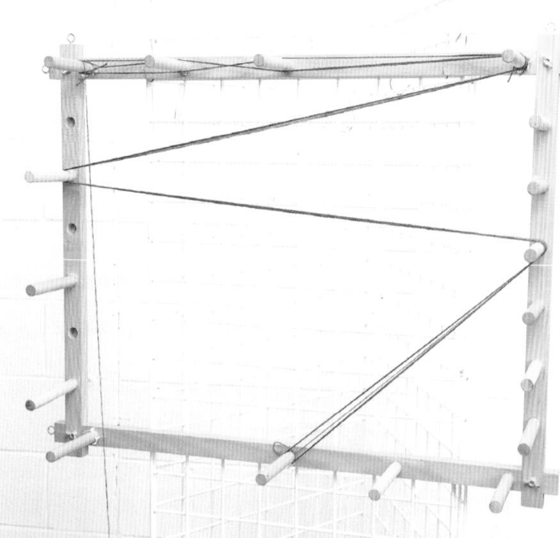

4. Now go to the next peg, passing the guide thread over it; then pass it under the next peg. Now move to the far right side of the board and go around the top peg. Next take the thread to the left side of the board and take it around the first peg.

5. Keep moving back and forth between the two sides, going around the next peg down each time, until you come to the end of your guide thread. Tie the guide thread to the nearest peg; any sort of knot will do just fine. Most warping boards are one yard across. This makes it so easy to wind and count especially if you are measuring your warp in lengths rounded to the nearest yard. This warp in our example is a 3½ yard warp.

■ TIPS

As you wind the warp:

- Be careful not to wind the warp too tightly. The warp should have a little give and not be tight like it would be on the loom. If it is too tight it might bend or break the warping board.
- If you should come to a knot in the warp thread, back up to the nearest end peg, retie the knot, and cut away the excess thread. This will get the knot out of the middle of your warp.

- Count as you go. I use a counting tie that I wrap around and through the warp as I wind it. Place this tie toward the middle of the warp and not at the cross; there will be more than enough ties there later. I like tying in bundles of twenty threads. But that's just me and you can count in any number that makes sense to you. It doesn't really matter as long as you end up with the needed number of threads.

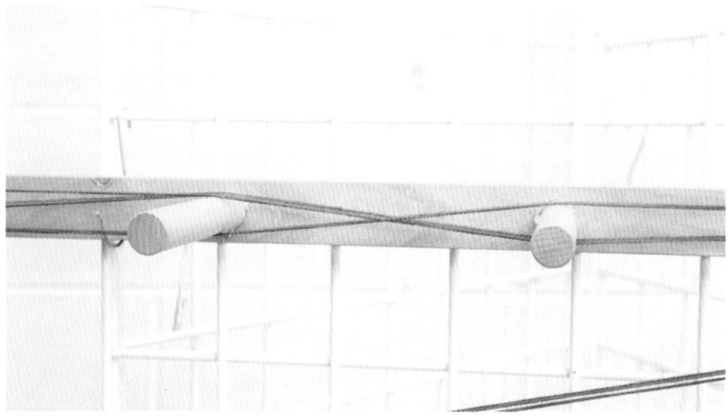

6 Now that the guide thread is on the board it is time to wind the actual warp. Tie the chosen warp thread to the first peg of the warping board. Take it through the cross, going over and under these next pegs just like you did with the guide thread, and then continue to follow the guide until you reach the last peg and the end of the guide thread. Go around this peg (it doesn't matter whether you go over or under this one).

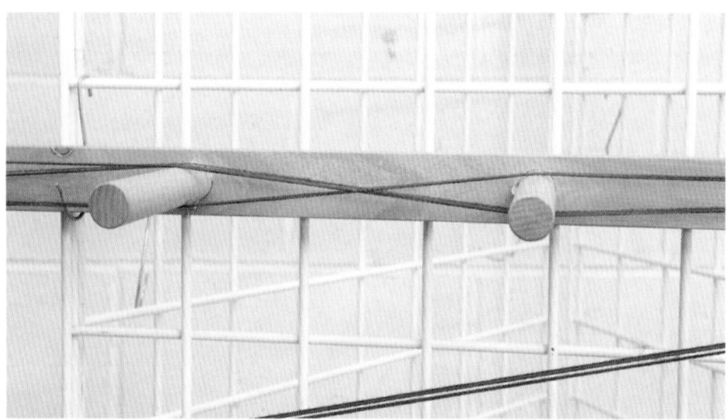

7. Now follow the path back toward the cross. When you get to the cross, go *over* the first peg and *under* the next (the opposite of how you started out), and then out to the peg where you tied on at the beginning. Go around this peg and continue along the same path from beginning peg to the ending peg, following the same route as before.

8. When you have the number of threads you need, place a number of ties throughout the warp to secure it and keep it neat. The first tie to make is the cross tie. Locate the cross in the beginning of the warping board and look at the figure eight. With a piece of cord that is thicker and a different color from the warp, go in from the front on one side of the cross, around the back, and back out on the other side to wrap the cord around the center of the cross. Tie a knot at the end of the cord, making a large loop rather than a tight tie. Don't include the guide thread. That will stay on the warping board when you remove the warp later. Now put several more ties throughout the warp.

9. You are now ready to remove the warp from your warping board. Start at the bottom of the warping board and carefully remove the end loop from the peg. Put your hand through the loop, then grab the warp above the tie that forms the top of the loop and pull it through the loop to make a new loop. Think of your hand like a large crochet hook (and you are chaining with the warp thread).

10. Repeat the process again and again, working your way up the length of the warp and stopping just a few feet from the cross. Pull the cross free from the warping board. Be very careful not to pass the end of the warp through the last loop. This will lock the warp. If you want to secure the warp, simply tie another cord around the entire end, as shown here.

Sleying the Reed

You are now ready to sley the reed. This is the process of putting the warp threads into the reed in their proper and chronological order. We will be using a 12 dent reed.

1. Start by finding two long, flat sticks that will reach from the front beam of the loom to the back beam of the loom. They should extend over the beams just a little so they don't slip and drop off the beams.

Lay the reed down on the sticks, which will support the reed as you sley the warp into it.

2. Place the warp's cross on the front beam and undo its chain over the loom's harness frames and back to the back beam of the loom. Wrap the warp around the back beam and tie it tightly to the beam, to prevent the warp from shifting while you work in the front, sleying the reed.

3. From the front of the loom, transfer the cross to a pair of lease sticks. Place a stick on either side of the cross (currently secured by the cord you put there when you made the warp on the warping board).

Secure the ends of the lease sticks either with a cord or, my favorite method, with ring binders.

Untie the cords that secured the cross in the warp. You do not need them now because the warp is now safe on the lease sticks.

4. Slide the lease sticks back toward the castle of the loom and place them on the sticks that hold the reed in place. The lease sticks should now be located between the reed and the castle of the loom. You should have a long length of the warp extending from the lease sticks toward the front of the loom. This is the portion of the warp that you will be sleying into the reed.

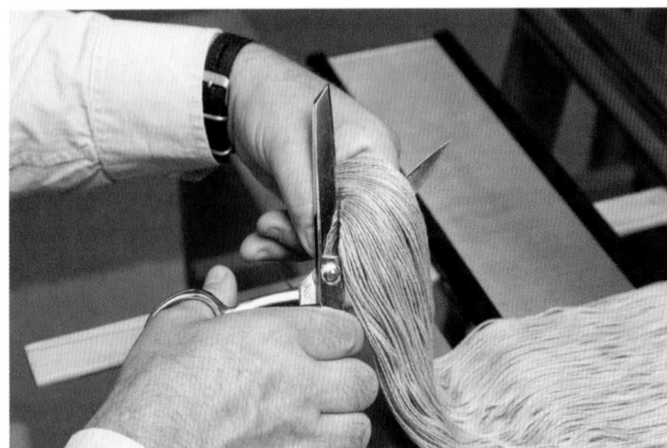

5. Be brave and cut through the end of your warp.

6. To get ready to sley the warp you need to make a few measurements. Start by finding the center of your reed and mark it. Next find the spot on the reed where you need to start the warp (I am right handed so I like to start on the right side of the reed and work across the reed to the left; if you are left handed you may prefer to start on the left side of the reed). Lay the tape measure back on the reed and measure half the width of the warp out from the center. Since our warp was wound with 300 total ends, and is to be sleyed at 12 EPI for 25 inches wide, I need to measure out 12½ inches to the right of the center.

■ WINDING A SECTIONAL BEAM

If you have a sectional warp beam, you will wind the warp onto it one section at a time. Use a spool rack with a spool of thread for each thread needed per section, then thread the warp through a tension box. Place the tension box on the back beam of the loom, directly above the section that is to be wound. Attach the warp threads to the warp beam by tying them to the cord that comes up from each section. As you wind the warp, you need to calculate the number of turns needed to achieve the desired length of the warp (based on the circumference of your warp beam). When you have finished winding the section, cut the warp free, secure the ends, and move on to the next section. Winding the warp sectionally allows you to warp your loom with much more warp than you would be able to do with conventional chain warping.

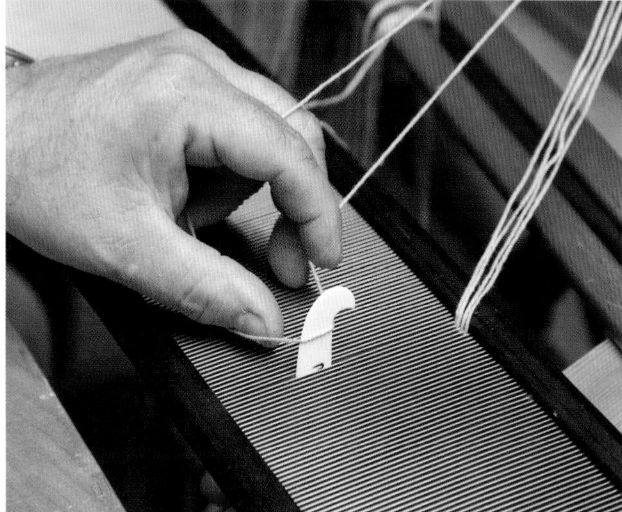

7. Take a sleying hook in your right hand. Bring the hook up from the bottom of the reed. Pull the first warp thread on the right-hand side off the lease sticks, place it in front of the hook, and pull it down through the reed.

Work across the reed, sleying it with one thread per dent. When you are finished you will have the warp centered in the reed (with 12½ inches to the right and left of the center, in our 25-inch example). I like to tie the warp threads that I have sleyed in 1 inch bundles under the reed with a slip knot. That way, if the reed should get bumped and fall off the sticks, your work is saved.

Threading the Heddles

Your next step is to thread the heddles.

1. Untie the warp from the back beam and bring the chain warp forward and over the harnesses to the very front of the loom.

2. Hold the reed in one hand and, with the other, remove the sticks that supported the reed. Flip the reed and place it in the beater of the loom so that the sleyed warp ends are facing toward the castle of the loom and the harnesses. Adjust the warp ends so that there are approximately 12 to 14 inches of warp coming through the reed. This should be enough warp length to thread through the heddles.

3. Wrap the warp chain around the front beam of the loom and tie it securely. This will prevent the warp threads from shifting and pulling as you thread them through the heddles, keeping them all the same length and helping to prevent tangles in the warp later on.

4. Go to the back of the loom at this point and look at your loom. Is there any way that the loom can be folded up to make getting to the heddles any easier? Some looms have a back beam that is removable. Your loom may also be able to fold up to the castle, allowing you to get very close to the harness frames and heddles. If your loom does have a folding option, be sure to use it. It will make threading easier and save you from having to stretch your arms out for hours at a time. I like to use a low, comfortable stool that lets me sit with the heddles nearly at eye level. If your loom is a Jack-type loom, where the harnesses raise up to make the shed, use a block of wood, a cone of yarn, or a book standing on its end to raise the harnesses up and bring them to your eye level.

Counterbalance and countermarch looms' harness frames are already raised slightly because they are suspended from cords coming down from rollers or jacks at the top of the loom.

5. Untie the first bundle of warp threads, bring them down and under the harness frames, and put them in your left hand.

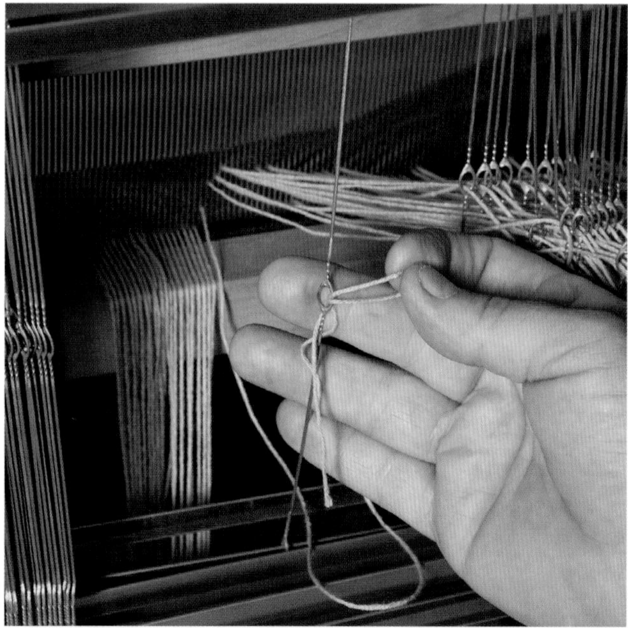

6. With your right hand, thread the first thread coming out from the reed. You want to take the threads in the same order they were sleyed in. Fold the thread into a small loop and poke it through the heddle eye, being very careful that the thread goes in a straight path through the eye and doesn't get twisted.

7. Thread the heddles according to the threading draft and pattern. After you thread a bundle, be sure to retie it into a slip knot. Continue threading until you have come to the end, then unfold the loom and reassemble it to its original position. Don't forget to remove the blocks holding up the harness if you are using a Jack-type loom.

Tying the Threads to the Apron Rod

1. Bring the apron rod up and over the top of the back beam. It is very important to have the apron rod and cords going over the back beam because the warp needs to travel over the back beam and then down to the warp beam. This will keep the warp threads on a straight and horizontal plane, resulting in a good clear shed when you are weaving. Adjust the apron cord length so that you can tie onto the apron rod.

2. Untie the first bundle of threaded warps on the right-hand side and take them over the apron rod. Split them in half and bring one half up and around on the right and the other half up and around on the left of the bundle. Tie the two ends together with a square knot.

3. Now go the left side and do the same with the bundle on the far left. This will support the apron rod as you tie the rest of the warp to the rod.

4. Tie the rest of the warp threads onto the apron rod.

Winding the Warp onto the Warp Beam

1. Before you start to wind the warp onto the warp beam you must remember to go to the front of the loom and untie the warp from the front beam. After you do this you will want to use your hands and straighten out the warp and check for tangles.

2. Bring the beater forward and rest it against the front beam.

3. Go to the side of the loom and step on the break treadle to release the tension on the break cable. Locate the crank that moves the warp beam and turn it clockwise. This will wind the warp forward and onto the warp beam.

4. If the beater moves forward and rests against the castle of the loom, stop and untangle the warp or you risk tearing warp threads.

5. As you wind the warp onto the warp beam, be sure to separate the layers of warp by using sticks, heavy paper, or (my favorite) single-face corrugated cardboard. This will help to maintain an even tension on the warp.

6. Stop after every couple of turns and pull on the warp chain in the front of the loom. This will help you keep a tight warp and prevent the cardboard from slipping. If you have a friend hold onto the warp as you wind it, that can be helpful too—but you can certainly do this task all by yourself. Wind the warp until the end of the warp chain is at the front beam and then stop.

Tying onto the Front Apron Rod

1. Locate the take-up mechanism on the cloth beam. This is usually on the right side and is called the ratchet and pawl. Release it so the cloth beam will turn and allow the apron rod to come up over the front beam and stop just beyond the beam.

2. Cut through the end of the warp. You can do this by cutting through the loop ends with your scissors or by simply cutting straight across the end.

3. You will now have hundreds of individual ends that need to be secured. Tie them in large bundles or take the time to count out each inch worth of warp and tie these in individual bundles using a slip knot.

4. Starting on either the right or left, begin tying the warp to the apron rod, an inch worth of warp threads at a time. Take them over the apron rod and down around the bar, then split the bundle into two equal parts and bring them back up around the outside of the original bundle. Tie the first part of a square knot with the two small bundles.

5. Now move to the opposite side of the warp and repeat step 4 with the first inch's worth of warp threads on that side.

6. Continue going back and forth from side to side, tying one-inch bundles of warp to the apron rod, only securing each bundle with the first half of a square knot.

7. When you reach the middle and tie the last half square knot, pull up on it firmly and then tie the second portion of the square knot to complete it. Feel the tension of the knot. This is what you want the rest of the knots to feel like.

8. Working from side to side again, complete the other knots, pulling up on them and bringing them to the same tension as the center knot before tying them off. As I tie the second half of each square knot, I take the tails of warp thread and poke them down on the side of the knot to help myself keep track of which knots are completed.

9. When you have finished tying the knots, take a moment and gently press down on the warp threads to feel if the tension seems even. If not, go back and redo the knots that need to be adjusted.

10. When every knot feels the same, you may want to add additional tension to the warp before you start to weave. Use the ratchet and pawl to tighten the warp. Don't make it too tight, though, or you won't be able to get a shed when you step on the treadle. If the warp is too tight, readjust your tension by taking the pawl back one notch or by gently depressing the break assembly.

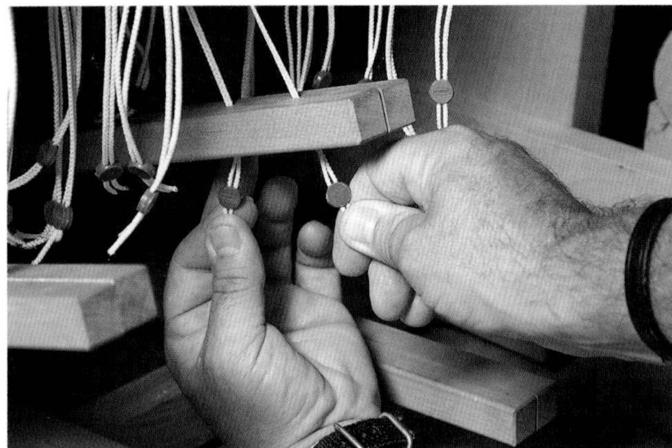

11. If you haven't tied up the treadles until now this is a good time to do it so you can check the shed. Many four-harness looms have six treadles. This allows you to have two tabby treadles and four twill treadles. The tie-up arrangement can be any way you like. Some weavers will place the tabby treadles on the far outside and tie the four twill treadles in the middle; others tie the twill treadles on the left-hand side and the last two treadles to weave tabby. Any way that pleases you will work. The tabby treadles are tied up as follows: One treadle should be tied to lift harnesses 1 and 3, and the second tabby treadle should lift harnesses 2 and 4. This allows you to alternate the odd numbered harnesses against the even numbered harnesses. The four twill treadles should be tied to lift harnesses 1 and 2, 2 and 3, 3 and 4, and 1 and 4, respectively.

When this job is done you are ready to step on the treadles to see if you have a clear shed (if not, adjust the warp tension, as described in step 10).

Congratulations! You have warped your loom and are ready to weave. Now that wasn't so bad, was it?

CHAPTER 5

Weaving a Rag Rug

You are now ready to start weaving your rug!

Well, you are almost ready. Take a look at where the warp ends are tied to the apron rod. The knots force the warp ends into a lot of little V formations. This is the way it's supposed to be, but it's not a great way to start off your weaving—you want the warp to be spaced evenly in your rug, and it's not right now. To even out the warp, you'll weave some waste material (maybe some cheap old yarn) into the warp for about an inch or more in plain weave. This evens out the warp and creates a firm base to start your rug from. This waste material will be cut out after the rug is woven, when you begin to do the finishing.

Ah! The finishing is something you need to think about right now. Do you want to have fringe on your rug, or will you simply roll a hem on each end? Fringes look beautiful and are the expected finish for a rug, but a rolled hem makes washing the rug much easier because fringes get tangled in the wash. In the next chapter, we will talk more about how to finish your rug, but the reason we are having all this talk about finishes now is because how you plan to finish your rug makes a big difference in where you place the waste material at the beginning. If you are planning on doing a rolled hem, you can start weaving the waste material just above the knots where you tied the warp to the apron rod (leave about an inch or so above the knots for a little ease). If you are planning on a fringe, start weaving in the waste material about three inches above the knots. After you finish weaving the rug, when you remove it from the loom, you will untie the knots on the front apron rod. This length of the warp is going to be the fringe on this end. The remaining unwoven warp that makes up the loom waste at the other end will be for the fringe on the other end.

Before you start weaving in the waste material, check the tension of the warp. The tension that was put on the warp by tying it to the apron rod is usually not enough. The warp should be firm to the touch when you press down on it with an open hand. If you are weaving on a counterbalance or countermarch loom you can put even more tension on the warp because the warp threads will be moving in both directions, up and down, when you step on a treadle to make the shed. If you are using a jack loom, the warp should be slightly looser because the warp threads only move up when the shed is being made. If the warp is too tight you compromise the shed and it may be difficult to get a wide enough shed to get a shuttle through.

Weave the waste material with a tabby treadling. Weave the first row with the 1 and 3 tabby pick and the second row with the opposite 2 and 4 pick. Then beat the two picks together. By not beating after each tabby pick you close the gap much faster. Weave a few more picks the same way for an inch or so to make this firm foundation. Don't be concerned with how this section looks; remember that this is only the waste material.

If you are planning on using a temple (a stretcher that helps to maintain the width of your rug as you weave), you should place it on the waste now.

You are now ready to start weaving the heading for your rug. The heading is one of the most important parts of the rug because it provides a stable beginning and ending for your rug and prevents the rags from coming undone. On

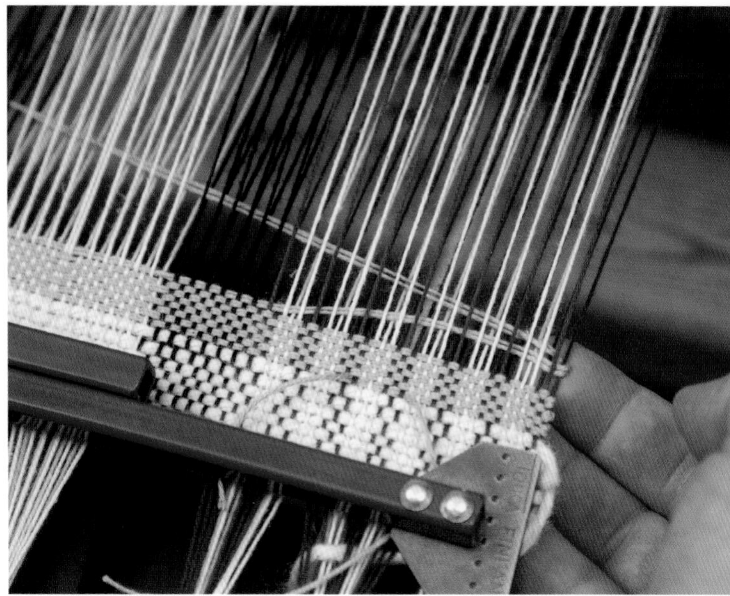

many commercially woven rag rugs that you find for sale in discount stores, the knots are tied directly up against the rags. This is poor construction: If for some reason the knots become untied, the rags will slip free and the rug will come apart. A heading eliminates this problem. If you want a rolled hem on your rug, you should allow several inches of heading so that you can roll the hem twice and stitch it in place. If you are planning on a fringed edge, weave only about ½ inch of heading at the beginning and at the end of your rug. At the beginning and end of the heading, take the ends of your weft around the last warp end and lay them back into the first and last picks of the heading.

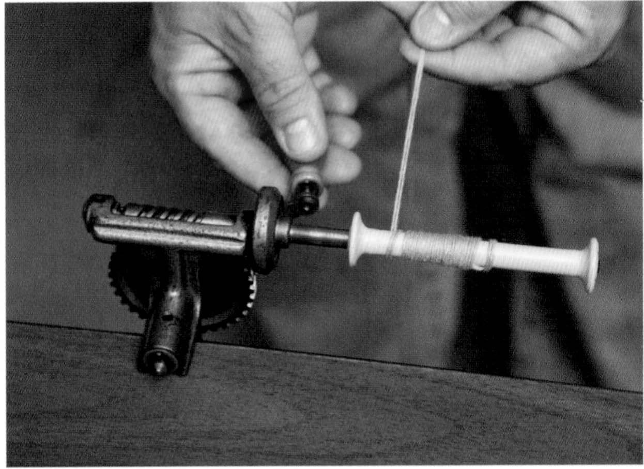

To prevent excess draw-in and later buckling in your rug, make an easy transition from the heading to the first pick of your rag weft. There is too much difference in size between a single strand of 8/4 cotton warp and a rag weft, so I use two strands of 8/4 cotton carpet warp wound together on a bobbin as the weft material for my headings.

In addition, I weave the heading material into the warp with a deliberate arch in the middle to introduce more of the weft material into the warp; this also helps with the draw-in.

If I'm going to be finishing a rug with a rolled hem, I weave the heading in one of two ways. The first is to weave the hem area in a simple tabby weave. The second method of weaving hem areas is something I adapted from instructions I found for weaving hems on dish towels and placemats. Look at the treadling instructions given here. You will see that there are places in the draft where the weft is doubled back into the same shed. This creates a double row and makes an obvious fold line. To make the double fold line simply take your shuttle around the last warp thread to lock it in place—or if you are using a floating selvedge, go around it—and then throw the shuttle back into the same shed. The two doubled lines will make it much easier to see where to fold the hem and to get straight lines. Also notice that the doubled rows are not evenly spaced in the treadling instructions: The area closest to the rug is wider than the area near the waste material. This helps to avoid extra build-up under the fold.

When you have finished weaving the beginning heading for your rug, you are ready to weave your first row of rags. Wind your rags onto a rug shuttle tightly, so as to wind on as much material as you can without the shuttle getting too bulky.

If the shuttle is overwound and bulging at the sides, you are going to have a difficult time getting it to pass smoothly through the open shed.

Make a 5- to 6-inch taper at the end of your rag strip with a pair of sharp scissors.

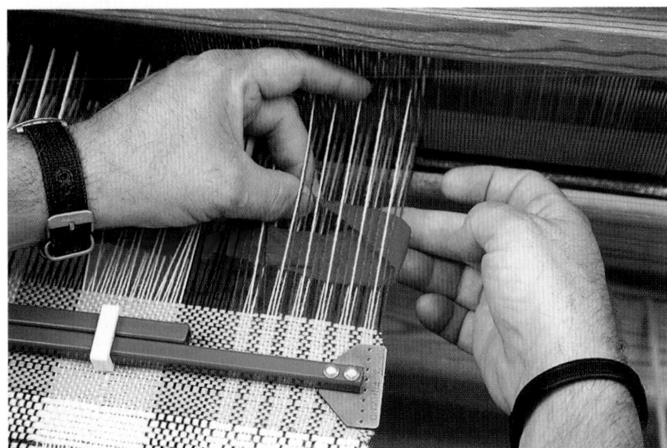

Following your treadling instructions, weave the first pick of rags across the warp, leaving approximately half the tapered end sticking out from the edge. Beat the rags into place. Open the same shed again and now wrap the tapered end back into the shed and beat again.

This will make a good-looking beginning selvedge, without a bulky build-up or a raw bit of rag hanging out.

Continue to weave the rags into your rug, following the treadling instructions. Here are some things to keep in mind as you go along:

• Make sure to angle the weft or arch the weft in the middle to prevent excess draw in.

• You also want to make sure you beat the rags firmly into place. I beat with an open shed first, then change to the next shed and beat again. This helps to pack the rags firmly into place and creates a tight rug that will wear well.

• If you are using a temple to help with the draw-in, be sure to move the temple forward every 1½ to 2 inches as you weave. Always move the temple first before you advance your warp. This will prevent any chance of the temple's sharp teeth from being dragged across the front breast beam and scratching it.

• Advance the warp frequently. This will go without saying as you start to weave. Rags weave up quickly, and you may get between 4 and 5 weft picks to the inch. After 3 to 4 inches of weaving you will notice that the shed is getting smaller and it is harder to get the shuttle through; advancing the warp will make the shed much wider again.

• Be mindful of how your selvedge edge looks. The edge of your rug will never be as neat or clean-edged as that of a dish towel or, for that matter, the fabric that you just bought and cut up to make this rug—it's simply impossible. Your weft is heavy cut strips of fabric, not thread, so it cannot make as smooth a selvedge edge. You can make the edge as smooth as possible, however, by using your fingers to place the bended strip neatly at each edge.

• When you get to the end of the shuttle's rags, it will be time to add a new shuttle. Cut the ends on a long taper, and it will be easy to overlap the tapers and get a nice neat splice.

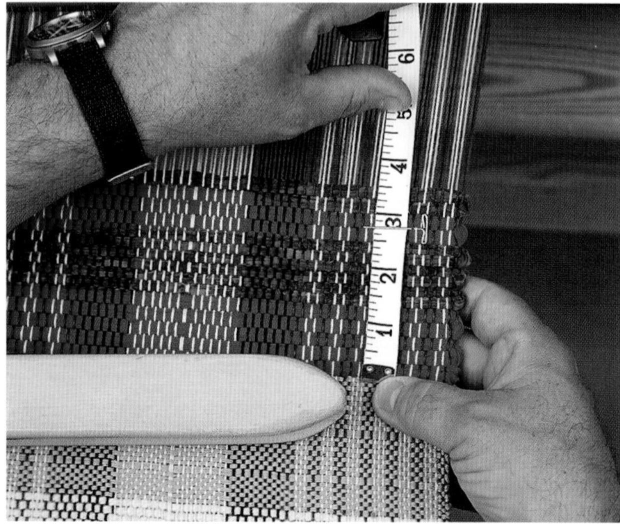

• Measure as you go so that you can keep track of how much you have woven. You can do this several ways. You can pin a tape measure to the beginning of your rug at the selvedge edge and just keep pinning it to the rug's woven surface as you go. You can also just measure as you weave and stick a pin in at the edge every foot or so, keeping track of how much you have woven.

• This brings up the point of how much to weave. Remember that the warp on the loom is under tension. When the rug is removed from the loom it will relax and tighten up, getting shorter. On average, I weave 14 inches on the loom for each 12 inches of finished rug I want. So a rug that needs to be 60 inches finished will be woven 70 inches long on the loom. Of course, there are always exceptions. Always, always, always allow yourself to be open to the fact that the rug might not come out exactly to the measurement that you want it to be. It is a rag rug, after all, and not a quilt patch that needs to fit precisely. If the rug doesn't fit the way you want it to in the place where you thought it should go, you can find another place for it. Sometimes I warp the loom with the whole intention of just weaving up the rags I have on hand: When the rags run out, the rug is done. Or I weave until I come to the end of my warp, regardless of how many rags I have left to weave. I can always add them to my stash and use them in another rug sometime. There are far greater things to worry about than the exact measurement of a rag rug. Live freely and weave happy!

When you get to the end of your rug, finish it in the same manner in which you started it. Let the rag weft extend out from the selvedge edge about 5 inches and cut it off. Then open the shed and back the rag out a little bit so that you can cut it at a taper. Once the end is tapered, wrap the end around the last warp end and put it back into the shed, using just your fingers to manipulate it into place.

When you are pleased with the way the selvedge looks, beat the weft again to lock it into place. Next, weave the ending heading so it matches the beginning heading.

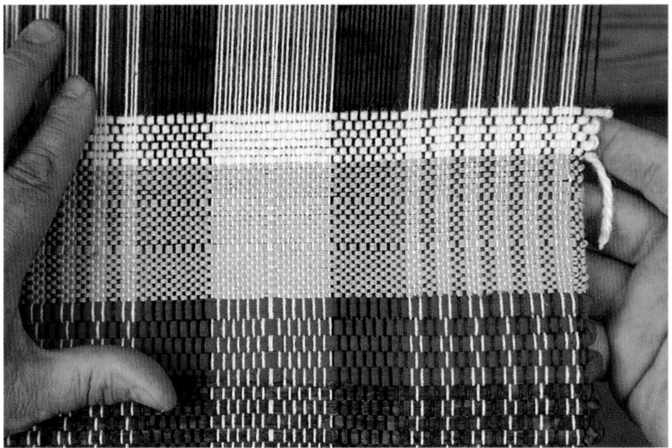

Hold on! You are not ready to take the rug off the loom just yet. Finish by weaving some waste material right up next to the final heading.

This way, when the rug is cut free from the loom and untied from the front apron rod, it is in a stable condition. You could leave it just the way it is for a long time without the fear of the headings unraveling.

There are two ways you can remove the rug from the loom. If you have warped your loom for just the one rug, then you can safely cut the warp behind the harness frames. This will give you about 12 to 14 inches of warp extending out beyond the final waste material that you can use for the fringe of your rug. When you untie the knots in the front, that warp length will be the fringe for the other side of the rug. If you have planned on a hem and no fringe is wanted, then you can cut the warp somewhere between the waste material and the reed. At the other end, you will cut the warp ends between the knots and the waste material section.

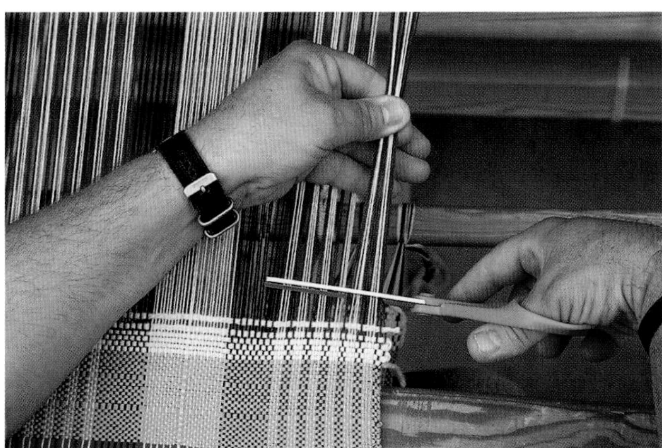

But perhaps you have warped your loom for several rugs and want to take this one off the loom right now and finish it. In this case you want to be careful not to lose the ends of warp from the reed and harnesses as you remove the rug from the loom. Advance the warp so that the heading and waste material are over the warp beam, plus enough warp length for a fringe if that's how you're finishing it.

Relax the tension on the warp. This will help prevent the warp ends from flying back through the reed as you cut them. I like to count and cut the warp ends in one-inch sections; as I cut the ends, I immediately tie them into slip knots. This prevents them from slipping through the dents in the reed.

Work your way across the warp, counting threads, cutting them, and tying them into slip knots.

Then untie the knots at the front of the loom and remove the rug.

When you are all finished, take a moment to look at your new rug for the first time. Put it on the floor and admire it the way it's intended to be admired. Until now, you have been looking at your rug from between waist height and eye level for all the time that you have been weaving. Now you can see your rug from standing height. Doesn't it look different? All of a sudden, the selvedge edges are much more acceptable, at five feet or more away from your eye. Clap your hands together and do the Happy Weaver Dance. (But not *on* your rug just yet, because you see you haven't hemmed the rug or tied fringes so far.) Congratulations on a rug well woven!

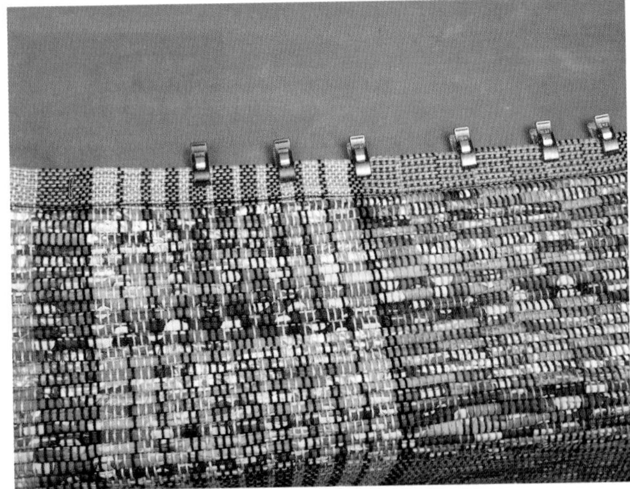

Next, with a tapestry needle and strong thread, sew the edge of the hem down. To be sure you have enough thread to go across the rug, measure out about twice the width of the rug. With your threaded needle, go behind the first warp thread and then into the fold of the hem fabric.

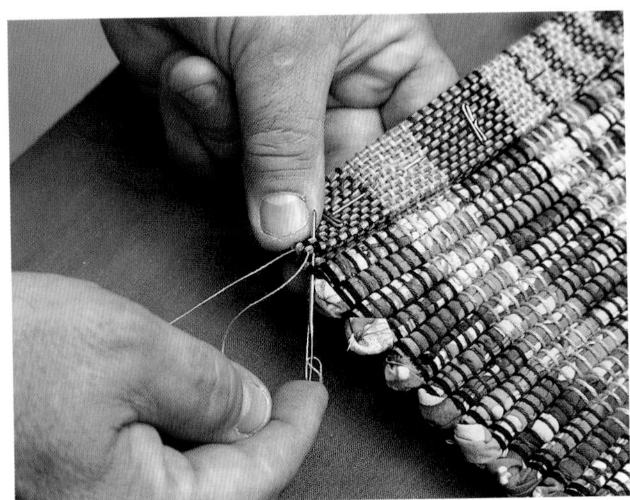

Pull the thread through, leaving 6 inches of the thread hanging out at the end. Go back up and catch the next warp end, then go back down into the hem and pull tightly.

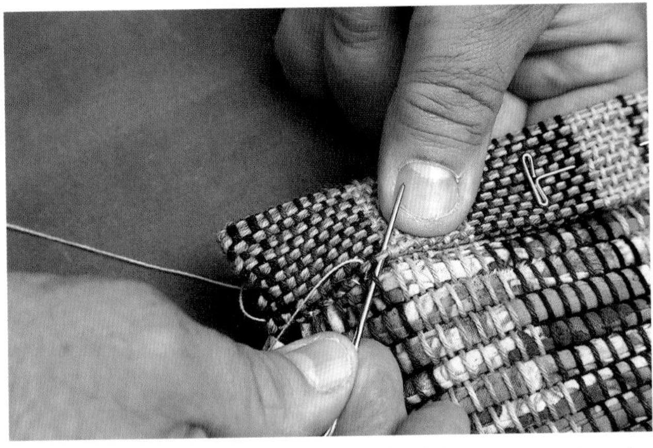

Continue to work across the rug in this way, securing the hem. Remove the T-pins or clips as you go to make the sewing easier.

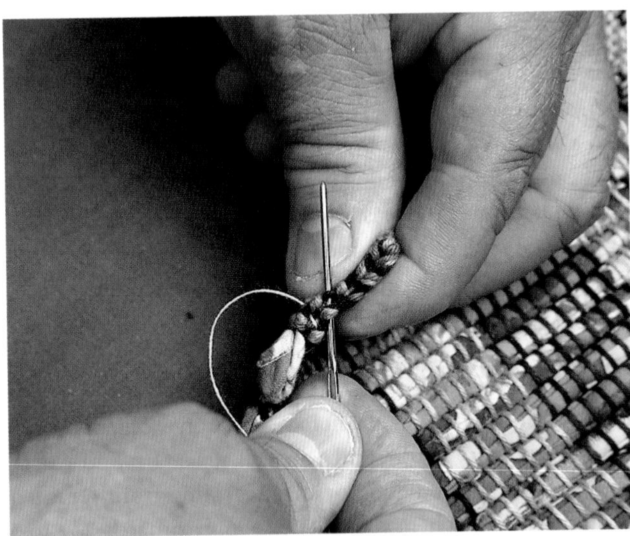

When you get to the end of your rug, close up the hem's edge with a simple overcast stitch.

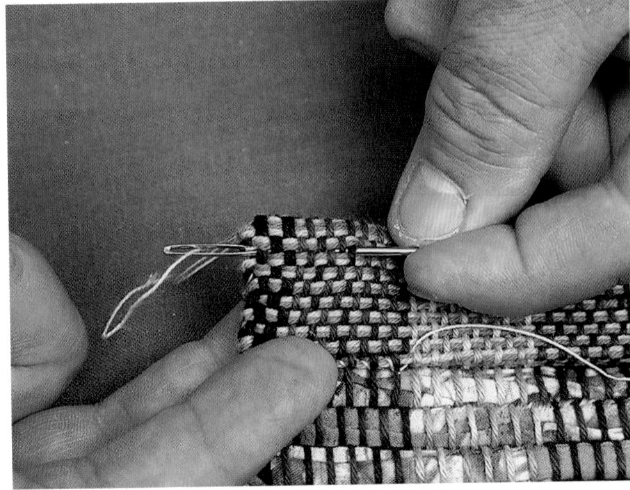

Then take the needle and push it into the hem for about 2 inches before bringing it out, to bury the end of the thread in the interior of the hem.

Trim the thread up close to the hem. Close up the other end in the same way with the 6-inch tail you left at the beginning.

Finishing with a Fringe

If you want to give your rug a fringed edge, then you will start by laying it on a table, with the edge of the rug and the waste material right at the table's edge. Place something heavy on the rug to keep it from sliding around as you work. You can use an old cast-iron pan or similar heavy object, or you can hold the rug down with a board and two C-clamps. With the rug in place at the table's edge, lay the board on top of the rug. The board needs to be a few inches longer than the rug is wide so that it can extend beyond the rug's selvedge and make a place to attach the C-clamps. Put the C-clamps on each end of the board (you can protect the underside of the table with a piece of folded cardboard) and tighten them down until the rug cannot move.

You are now ready to start tying overhand knots along the edge of your rug. I am right handed, so the photos that illustrate this process will all be working from right to left, but you can accomplish the same task moving from left to right if this is a more comfortable orientation for you.

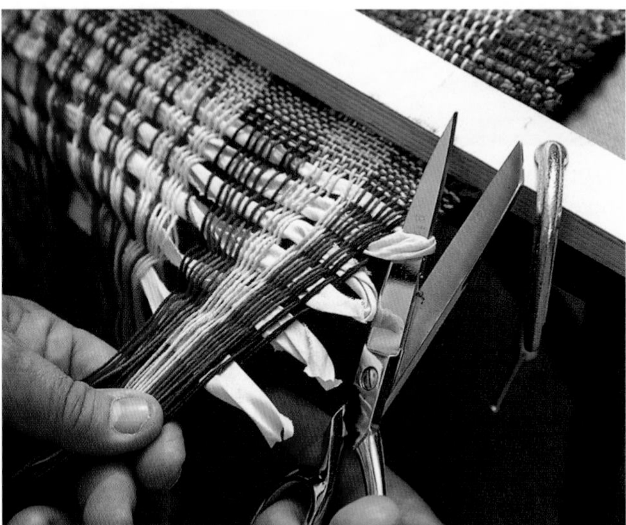

Start by carefully snipping the loops in the selvedge of the waste material. This will make removing the waste material much easier. *Do not remove all the waste material right away.* You are going to take it out a little at a time. If you pull it all out right away you will have nothing there to hold the heading in as you work.

Let's just take a moment to think about the size of the knots. If there are too many warp ends in the knot, then it becomes bulky and the finished edge of the rug looks out of proportion to the rest of the rug. I use approximately half an inch of warp threads per knot. I try to always have an even number of warp ends making up the knot. It would be nice if all the knots had the same number of ends in them, but because of the design of the rug, it doesn't always work out this way. You might have a few knots with more or fewer warp ends in them. Oh well, that's just the way it works out sometimes—and no one will notice when the rug is on the floor. If you have used floating selvedges in the rug, include them into the first and last knots.

The most commonly used knot for fringes is an overhand knot. There are two ways to go about making these knots. The first is to simply count out the next group of threads, removing the waste material from them; make a large loop with the threads, pull the tails through the loop, slide the loop up close to the rug's edge, and tighten the knot by pulling on the tails of the warp ends.

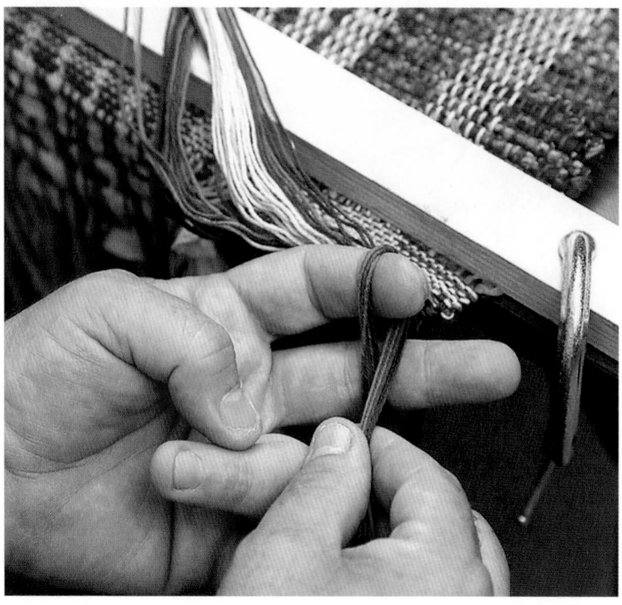

A second variation that I like a little better is to exchange the last warp thread from each group of threads with the first warp thread from the next group of threads. The crossing of these two ends helps to close the gap between the knots.

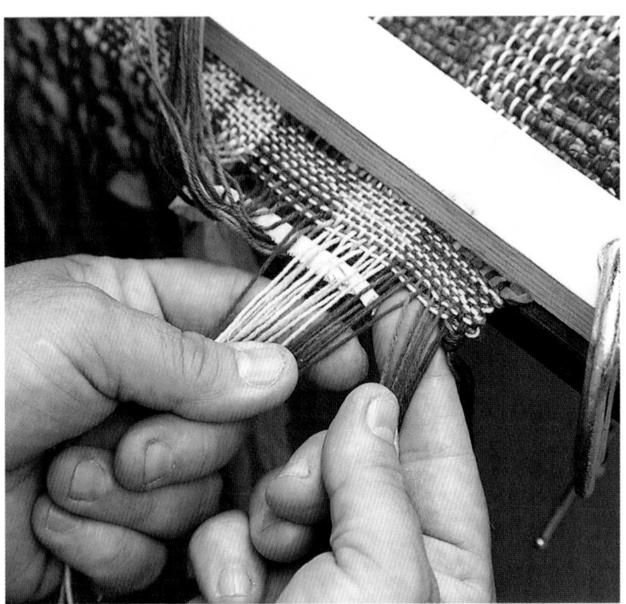

Crossed warp ends

When you have finished tying the knots on both ends of your rag rug, it's time to trim the fringe. The length of the fringe is a matter of personal choice. I prefer to have a fringe that's about 3 to 4 inches long. This is short enough that the fringe rarely gets tangled; it is also easy to shake out or comb the fringe so it looks nice and neat on the floor. To cut the fringe to an even length you can lay the rag rug on a table with the knotted edge 3 to 4 inches from the table's edge. Then, with a sharp pair of scissors, cut the fringe nice and straight.

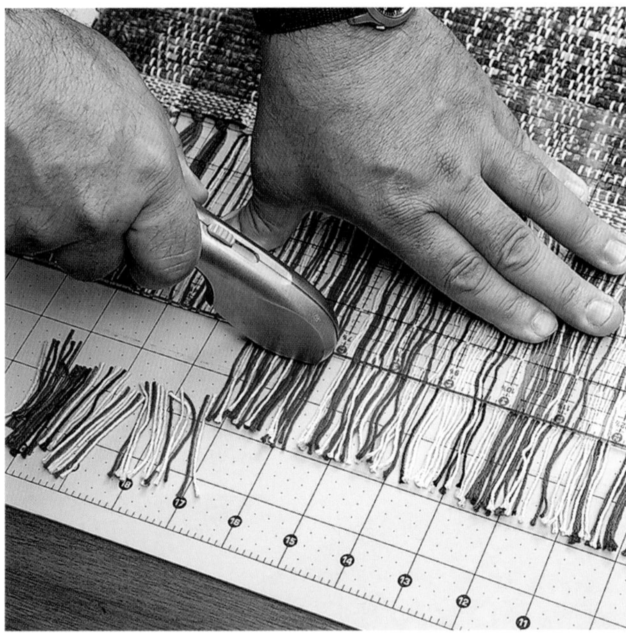

If you have a rotary cutter with a guide and self-healing mat, you can use them to easily cut a nice, straight fringe. Lay the rug on the mat, lining up the edge of the rug with the mat's grid. Straighten out the rug's fringe with a comb or hairbrush. Then lay the clear plastic guide on the fringe and line it up along the length where you want to make your cut. Apply a little pressure on the guide so it doesn't shift, and use the rotary cutter to cut along the guide, moving away from you. Then turn the rug around and do the other side.

There now! Your fringed rug is finished and ready to put on the floor and enjoy for years to come.

Finishing With a Damascus Edge

Another way of securing your heading's weft is to do a Damascus edge. You sometimes find this edge on Oriental rugs. Damascus is in the Middle East, after all, so the name makes perfect sense. All that trivia aside, this style of finishing makes for a tight, strong edge that is decorative as well. It's also a lot of fun to do.

A Damascus edge is nothing more than a series of half hitches. Start just the same way as you would to make an overhand knot, by removing the waste material from a small section of warp threads. Working from the right side, take the first warp thread on the right and place it on top of the next warp thread to its left. We will refer to this first thread as the active thread because it is the one that is moving. Take the end of the active thread behind the second thread and bring it up through the loop that was created.

Pull down on the second warp thread gently with your left hand. (This will be easy to do if you have the rug secured on the table with a heavy weight or the board and C-clamps.) Now pull up (toward the main body of the rug) on the active thread to tighten your knot. This is a half hitch knot.

Now repeat the process again, with the second warp thread becoming the new active thread and moving over and around the next thread to its left. Tie the knot in the same way as before and pull up tight. Continue this way all the way across the rug to the last warp end. Since there isn't another thread for this last thread to go around, we will just ignore it.

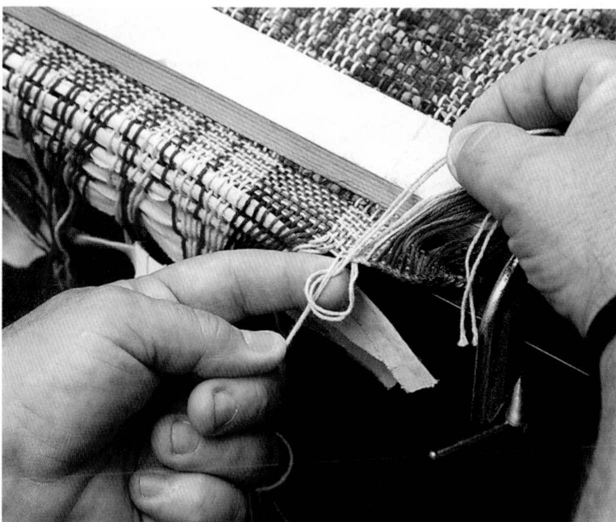

Take a look at the edge of your rug. You will notice that there is a braid on the bottom side of the rug's edge and all the warp ends with the exception of the last end are lying on top of the rug. The edge that you have just done is known as a half Damascus edge. To complete the edge treatment and

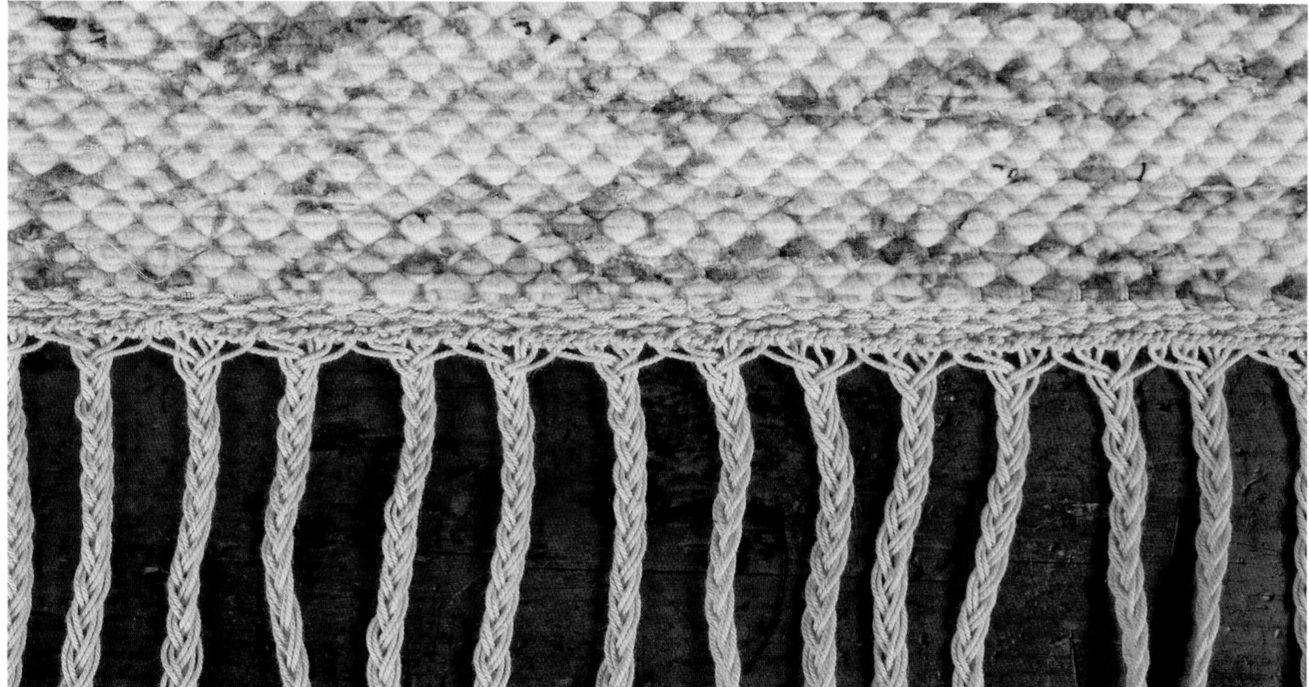

A Damascus edge with braided fringe—time-consuming but beautiful!

make it a full Damascus edge, turn the rug over and start again on the (new) right-hand side and repeat the whole process over again. The warp end that you couldn't use at the end on the first side will now be the first active thread on the second side.

When you have completed both sides of your rug you will have a braided edge on both sides of the heading, with the warp threads coming out of the center of the braided edge. At this point you can trim the fringe as you would for an ordinary fringed rug (or twist or braid the fringe, as described below).

The Damascus edge is a slow process, but it is a lot of fun to do. It results in a secure edge, with no need to fear that the heading will come out; it is also very pretty to look at. Because it is slow to do, you will not find this type of finishing being done on a rug for a commercial market. Do it for yourself or for a very special friend who will appreciate your efforts.

The Other Side of Finishing: Protecting the Warp

Up to this point, we have been talking about protecting the weft of your rug. Now I would like to address the idea of protecting the warp threads from disintegrating from the wear of walking and washing. Please do not panic, thinking your rug's beautiful fringe is going to fall apart right away. It won't, especially if you have used a cotton-polyester blend thread for your warp.

You can protect your fringe by doing some additional finishing on it. I will sometimes make a three-strand braid with my fringe. Divide the fringe into bundles and then make a braid from each bundle the same way you would braid someone's hair. Braiding takes up some of the threads' length, so take this into account and add in a little extra length when you trim the fringe. Braid the fringe to the desired length and then make an overhand knot on the end of the braid to keep it from coming undone. Braiding takes a great amount of time to do. I once timed myself and found it took me twice as long to finish the rug as it did to warp and weave it.

My all-time favorite way of finishing the fringe is to do a twisted fringe. I start by cutting my entire fringe to the same length, about 20 percent longer than I want my finished fringe to be. This will allow for the take-up that results from the twisting. The twist that builds up in the fringe will secure the edge of the heading, making it unnecessary to tie knots up against the heading first when doing a twisted fringe. If you have already tied knots or done a Damascus edge, however, that's perfectly fine. It's just more security. Sometime we switch directions in our thinking and decide to put a twisted fringe on our rug after tying all those knots. That is perfectly all right. It's good looking, it's secure, and your rug is just the way you want it to look, right? Right!

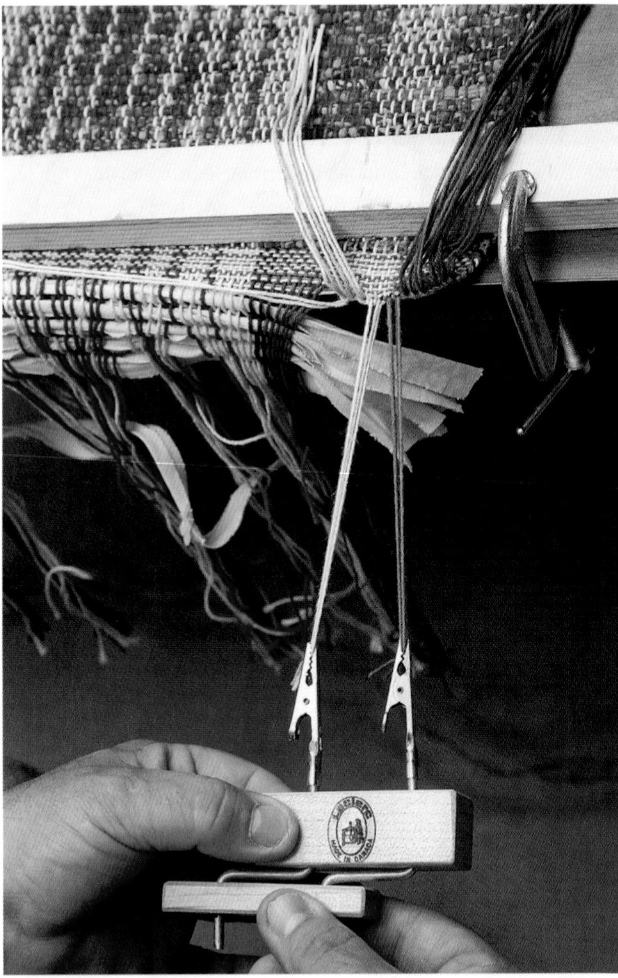

To make a twisted fringe, take two groups of threads and twist them in the same direction to build up tension and then let the groups twist back on each other in the opposite direction. You can do this by hand, but it is much faster and easier to do with a fringe twister. A fringe twister is made up of several alligator clips soldered onto some heavy wire and two blocks of wood that make up the body and handle.

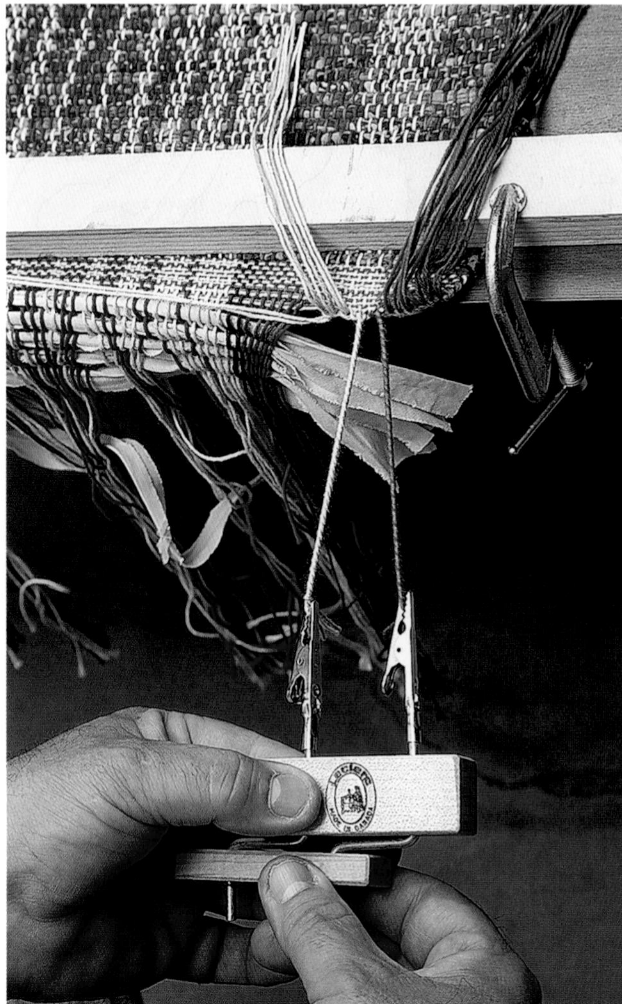

I suggest using half the number of warp ends for the twisted fringe as you had for the EPI. If your warp was set at 12 EPI, then use six ends of warp for the twisted fringe. When forming my groups, I cross the warp ends (as when tying knots for a fringe) to prevent gaps between the groups of twisted fringe. Place three warp ends in the teeth of one of the alligator clips and the other three warp ends in the teeth of the other alligator clip. Gently pull on the fringe twister to see if the groups need to be adjusted to make them even at the ends. Now hold the body of the twister in your left hand and with your right hand turn the handle to the right several times so you can see the twist building up. Count how many turns you are putting into your fringe. You want to turn it until the fringe seems to be noticeably overtwisted. You need this much twist in the fringe so it can balance itself out in the end. A 7-inch length of precut fringe may need 25 to 30 turns of the twister to create enough twist. Relax the fringe twister just a little, and see the two groups of warp kink up a little.

You are now ready to let the bundles twist back on themselves. This is so easy to do. Simply let the fringe twister fall down off the edge of the table. It will act like a counterweight and the fringe will automatically twist in the opposite direction.

After the fringe twister has slowed down and relaxed, undo the ends from the clips and immediately tie an overhand knot on the end of the twisted strand to secure it.

Repeat this all across the rug's edge. If your knots at the end are not all aligned up perfectly that is quite alright. Don't worry about it. As a matter of fact, one time I made all the knots fall at the exact same place and the knots crowded each other out, making the fringe splay outward. I had to redo the fringe by undoing every other knot and making them just slightly higher or lower than the knots on either side.

After Finishing

As you can see, there are a number of different ways to finish a rag rug. Some are more elaborate than others and some take more time to complete. In any of these cases, the whole idea is to make a finish that is appropriate for your rug and that will not only look good but will give your rug years on the floor for you to enjoy.

If after you have finished your rug and put it on the floor, you notice that there are waves and wrinkles in it, you can get rid of the waves by pressing the rug with a steam iron. Lay your rug on a firm surface like the floor. Place a damp towel on top of the rug and press it with a very hot steam iron. You could also take it to a cleaner, where they can put it on a large steaming press such as the type they might use to press slacks. For a small amount of money, your cleaner will do an exceptional job.

When considering the perfect place on the floor for the rag rug, be mindful of the flooring that it is going to be resting on. Tile and polished hardwood floors are slippery and may present a hazard for the people stepping on the rug. You don't want the rug to slide out from under someone and cause them to fall. Try placing a rubber mat under the rag rug to help it stay in place. You can purchase these mats at many stores that sell carpeting and Oriental rugs, or in many large national chain stores in their kitchen and bath areas. These mats look a lot like rubber-coated netting and are sometimes used for kitchen shelf liners.

Your rag rugs can take a lot of abuse, from being stepped on to frequent vacuuming. You can even take the rugs outside and hang them over a wash line or balcony railing and beat them with a broom or old-time carpet beater. When it comes down to washing them don't be frightened to put them into the washing machine for a good wash to get rid of any ground-in dirt or little gifts left behind by your pets. If your rug is too large to fit into the washing machine, you can put it into the bathtub with a 2 or 3 inches of warm soapy water and give it a good scrubbing with a nylon-bristle vegetable brush (like you might use to clean dirt off of potatoes). You could also put the rug over a picnic table or on a wooden deck and scrub it there. Just be sure to rinse it to get rid of all the excess soap from the wash water and then hang the rugs out to dry. You can dry rugs in a dryer, but I prefer to hang them outside on a sunny day.

CHAPTER 7

Projects

In this next section, you'll find a collection of rag rugs that I have designed for both plain weave and twill.

The inspiration for these designs came from numerous sources. The colors for the spice market rug came from a photograph of a vendor's stall in India. The warp-face rug, or "rainbow rug," as these rugs are known by antique dealers in the Mid-Atlantic area, was my attempt to reproduce a length of carpeting like the dozens of examples I have seen in shops and restored homes.

The rugs with gradations of colors are inspired by a car that belonged to a fellow student of mine back in high school. The front fender was one color and the rear fender another color. The blending of the two colors on the doors was nothing less than miraculous. By using stripes of different widths (which I now recognize as the Fibonacci mathematical series) the stripes in the front fender color got progressively narrower as they moved back toward the rear of the car and the stripes in the other color went from narrow to wider as you moved toward the rear fender. The car was *hot* and appeared to be moving even while it sat perfectly still in the parking lot.

The twill rugs section is one of my favorites. It shows patterns not often woven by contemporary weavers today. Although these rugs are not difficult to weave, they do require a little more concentration in the treadling. A Rose Path twill is a pattern that I have woven many times as toweling—so I thought, why not try it as a rag rug? The pattern is so pretty and the rug wears well in spite of the longer warp floats. Much of my inspiration in this section came from my research on rag rugs over the years. Some of my favorites have been the rag rugs that were woven in the first half of the last century: This seemed to be the heyday of the rag rug movement and quite a few of these rugs were woven in twill. Two of my favorites were the Hollywood Pattern and the Chicken Tracks. I have included these here, as well as a few variations on the Anderson Weave rug.

Sometimes the fabric that you have will be enough inspiration for the rugs you want to weave. The fabric colors might be perfect and all you have to do is choose the warp color or colors.

I hope you enjoy looking at this collection of rugs and are tempted to weave a few of your own. Be daring and change the colors and fabrics to fit the room or recipient the rug is intended for.

For all the single rugs I made a warp of 3 ½ yards long. This was usually long enough to weave a finished rug measuring 68 to 80 inches, depending on the fabric I was using. Many of the rugs used a single fabric for the rags. I simply bought between 8 and 10 yards of fabric, prepared it all into nice long rag strips, and wove until they ran out. At that point I was done, regardless of how long the rug turned out to be. This was a very easy way to go about it, but if you need to be a bit more precise, see chapters 2 and 4 for information on how to calculate the warp and weft you need to achieve a specific size of rug. Weave up a sample in your chosen fabric for extra precision. But above all, have fun with what you weave!

Old Glory Check

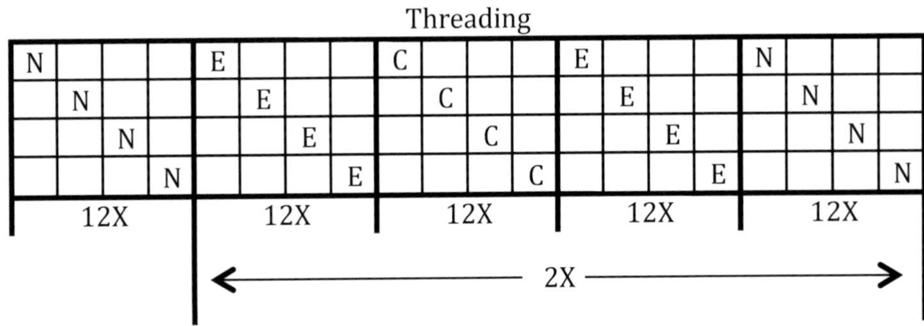

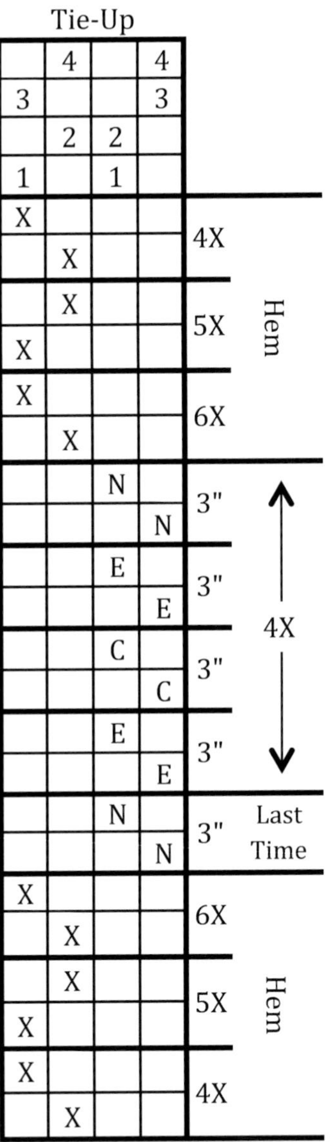

Warp #1

WARP
8/4 Cotton carpet warp

Colors
Dark Navy (N)
Ecru (E)
KY Cardinal (C)

Sett
16 EPI
2 per dent in an 8-dent reed

Width in Reed
27"

WEFT
Hems
2 strands of 8/4 cotton wound together as one

Rug Body
Cotton fabric in:
Navy (N)
Natural/Ecru (E)
Bright Red (C)

Strip width
Cut to 1 ½"-wide strips

Old Glory Variation

Threading

N				E				C				E				N			
	N				E				C				E				N		
		N				E				C				E				N	
			N				E				C				E				N
12X				12X				12X				12X				12X			
				← 2X →															

Tie-Up

	4		4		
3			3		
	2	2			
1		1			
X				4X	Hem
	X				
	X			5X	
X					
X				6X	
	X				
X				Body of Rug	
	X				
X				6X	Hem
	X				
	X			5X	
X					
X				4X	
	X				

Warp #1

WARP
8/4 Cotton carpet warp

Colors
Dark Navy (N)
Ecru (E)
KY Cardinal (C)

Sett
16 EPI
2 per dent in an 8-dent reed

Width in Reed
27"

WEFT
Hems
2 strands of 8/4 cotton wound together as one

Rug Body
Cotton print fabric

Strip width
Cut to 1½"-wide strips

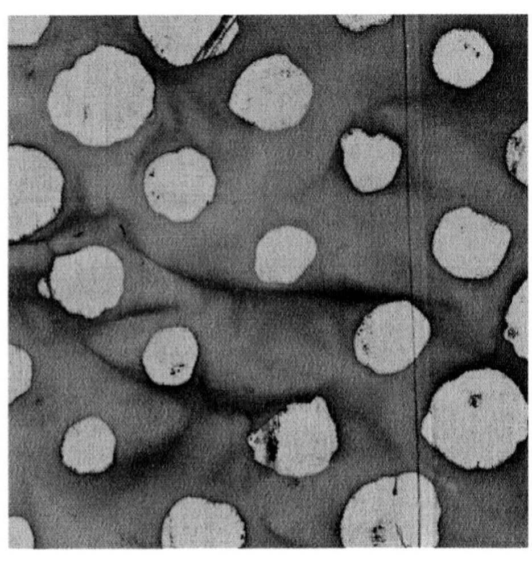

Lower Oven

Fog in the Glen

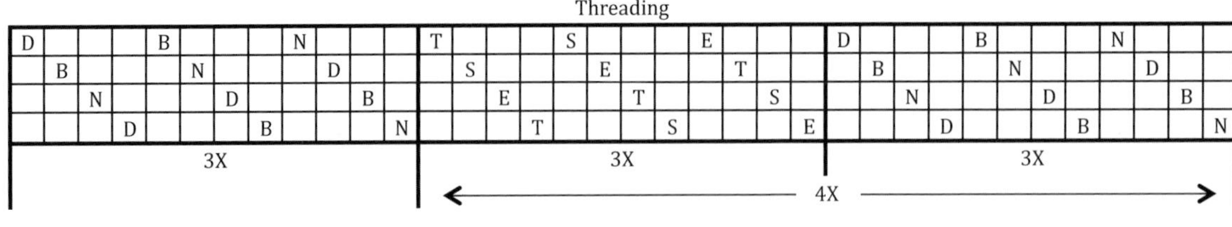

Tie-Up

	4	
3		
	2	
1		
X		4X (Hem)
	X	
	X	5X (Hem)
X		
X		6X (Hem)
	X	
X		Body of Rug
	X	
X		6X (Hem)
	X	
	X	5X (Hem)
X		
X		4X (Hem)
	X	

Warp #2

WARP
8/4 Cotton carpet warp

Colors
Navy (N)
Black (B)
Dark Brown (D)
Ecru (E)
Light Sage (S)
Tan (T)

Sett
12 EPI

Width in Reed
27"

WEFT
Hems
2 strands of 8/4 cotton wound together as one

Rug Body
Cotton print fabric

Strip width
Cut to 1½"-wide strips

Stormy Sky

Reed Sleying Profile Draft

N	12		10		8		6		4		2																								2		4		6		8		10		12
C		2		4		6		8		10		12		10		8		6		4		2		2		4		6		8		10		12		10		8		6		4		2	
R													2		4		6		8		10		12		10		8		6		4		2												

Threading

4				4				4			
	3				3				3		
		2				2				2	
			1				1				1

Tie-Up

	4		
3			
	2		
1			
X		4X	Hem
	X		
	X	5X	
X			
X		6X	
	X		
X		Body of Rug	
	X		
X		6X	Hem
	X		
	X	5X	
X			
X		4X	
	X		

Warp #3

WARP
8/4 Cotton carpet warp

Colors
Dark Navy (N)
Colonial Blue (C)
Royal Blue (R)

Sett
12 EPI

Width in Reed
25"

WEFT
Hems
2 strands of 8/4 cotton wound together as one

Rug Body
Cotton flannel

Strip width
Cut to 1½"-wide strips

Batik Bliss

Reed Sleying Profile Draft

N	12		10		8		6		4		2																								2		4		6		8		10		12
C		2		4		6		8		10		12		10		8		6		4		2		2		4		6		8		10		12		10		8		6		4		2	
R													2		4		6		8		10		12		10		8		6		4		2												

Threading

4				4				4			
	3				3				3		
		2				2				2	
			1				1				1

Tie-Up

	4		
3			
	2		
1			
X		4X	Hem
	X		
	X	5X	
X			
X		6X	
	X		
X		Body of Rug	
	X		
X		6X	Hem
	X		
	X	5X	
X			
X		4X	
	X		

Warp #3

WARP

8/4 Cotton carpet warp

Colors

Dark Navy (N)
Colonial Blue (C)
Royal Blue (R)

Sett

12 EPI

Width in Reed

25"

WEFT

Hems

2 strands of 8/4 cotton wound together as one

Rug Body

Cotton batik

Strip width

Cut to 1 1/2"-wide strips

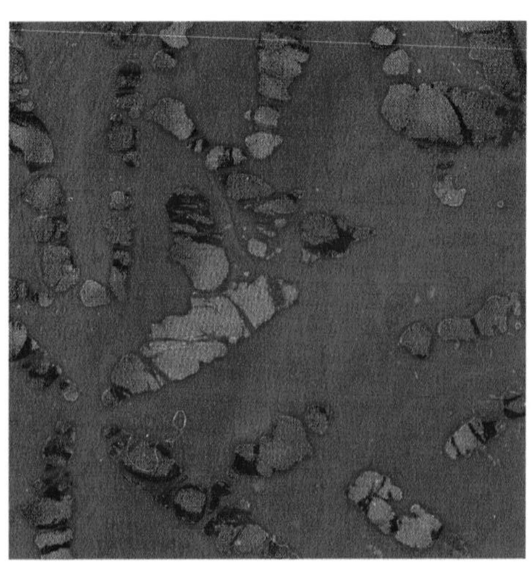

Rainbow Striped Rug with Log Cabin Background

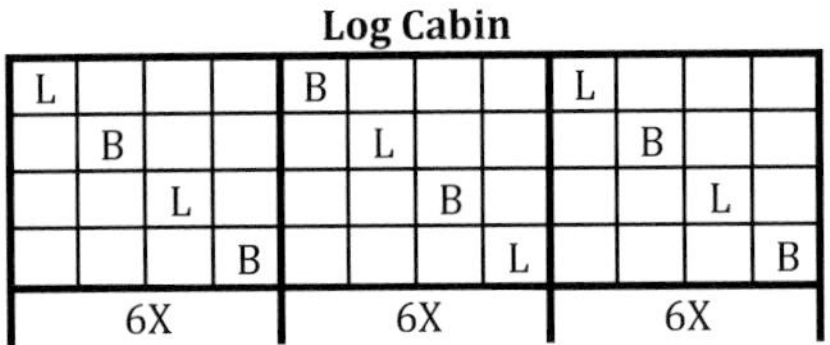

Log Cabin

L				B				L			
	B				L				B		
		L				B				L	
			B				L				B
6X				6X				6X			

Log Cabin Center Stripe

B				L				B			
	L				B				L		
		B				L				B	
			L				B				L
6X				6X				6X			
				← 3X →							

Log Cabin

L				B				L			
	B				L				B		
		L				B				L	
			B				L				B
6X				6X				6X			

Log Cabin	Rainbow Stripe	Log Cabin Center Stripe	Rainbow Stripe	Log Cabin
3"	6.5"	7"	6.5"	3"

Reed Sleying Profile Draft for Rainbow Color Stripe

Wine	12												12
Royal Blue		12										12	
Myrtle Green			12								12		
Lime				12						12			
Burnt Orange					12				12				
Red						12		12					
Cranberry							12						

Tie-Up

	4		
3			
	2		
1			
X		4X	
	X		
	X	5X	Hem
X			
X		6X	
	X		
X		Body of	
	X	Rug	
X		6X	
	X		
	X	5X	Hem
X			
X		4X	
	X		

Warp #4

WARP
8/4 Cotton carpet warp

Colors for Log Cabin
Dark Brown (B)
Linen (L)

Rainbow Color Stripe
Wine
Royal Blue
Myrtle Green
Lime
Burnt Orange
Red
Cranberry

Sett
24 EPI
2 per dent in a 12-dent reed

Width in Reed
26"

WEFT

Hems
2 strands of 8/4 cotton wound together as one

Rug Body
Cotton flannel

Strip width
Cut to 1½"-wide strips

Gradation Stripes 1

Left and Right Border Threadings

N				M				J				M				N			
	N				M				J				M				N		
		N				M				J				M				N	
			N				M				J				M				N
					3X				3X				3X						

Gradation Stripes

Dusty Rose	7		5		4		3		2		2		3		4		5		7
KY Cardinal		2		3		4		5		6		5		4		3		2	

Center Field

N				M				J				M				J				M				N			
	N				M				J				M				J				M				N		
		N				M				J				M				J				M				N	
			N				M				J				M				J				M				N
					3X				3X				3X				3X				3X						

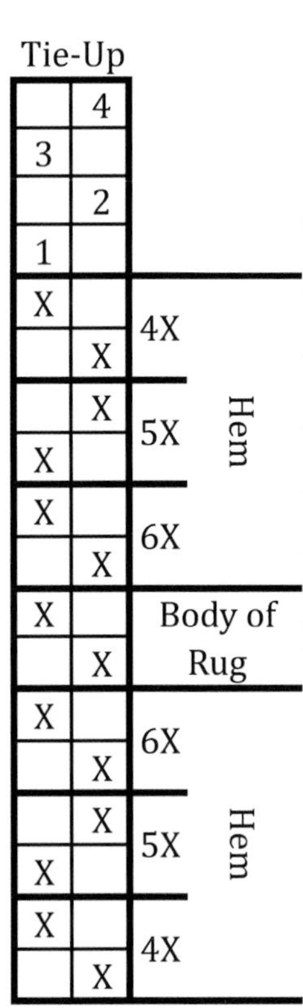

Warp #5

WARP

8/4 Cotton carpet warp

Colors

Navy (N)
Moody Blue (M)
Light Jade (J)
Dusty Rose
KY Cardinal

Sett

12 EPI

Width in Reed

25½"

WEFT

Hems

2 strands of 8/4 cotton wound together as one

Rug Body

Cotton fabric (solid wine-colored)

Strip width

Cut to 1½"-wide strips

Gradation Stripes 2

Left and Right Border Threadings

N				M				J				M				N			
	N				M				J				M				N		
		N				M				J				M				N	
			N				M				J				M				N
				3X				3X				3X							

Gradation Stripes

Dusty Rose	7		5		4		3		2		2		3		4		5		7
KY Cardinal		2		3		4		5		6		5		4		3		2	

Center Field

N				M				J				M				J				M				N			
	N				M				J				M				J				M				N		
		N				M				J				M				J				M				N	
			N				M				J				M				J				M				N
				3X				3X				3X				3X				3X							

Tie-Up

	4		
3			
	2		
1			
X		4X	
	X		
	X	5X	Hem
X			
X		6X	
	X		
X		Body of Rug	
	X		
X		6X	
	X		
	X	5X	Hem
X			
X		4X	
	X		

Warp #5

WARP
8/4 Cotton carpet warp

Colors
Navy (N)
Moody Blue (M)
Light Jade (J)
Dusty Rose
KY Cardinal

Sett
12 EPI

Width in Reed
25½"

WEFT

Hems
2 strands of 8/4 cotton wound together as one

Rug Body
Cotton fabric (solid jade green)

Strip width
Cut to 1½"-wide strips

Gradation Stripes 3

Left and Right Border Threadings

N				M				J				M				N			
	N				M				J				M				N		
		N				M				J				M				N	
			N				M				J				M				N
				3X				3X				3X							

Gradation Stripes

Dusty Rose	7		5		4		3		2		2		3		4		5		7
KY Cardinal		2		3		4		5		6		5		4		3		2	

Center Field

N				M				J				M				J				M				N			
	N				M				J				M				J				M				N		
		N				M				J				M				J				M				N	
			N				M				J				M				J				M				N
				3X				3X				3X				3X				3X							

Warp #5

WARP
8/4 Cotton carpet warp

Colors
Navy (N)
Moody Blue (M)
Light Jade (J)
Dusty Rose
KY Cardinal

Sett
12 EPI

Width in Reed
25½"

WEFT
Hems
2 strands of 8/4 cotton wound together as one

Rug Body
Cotton print fabric (polka dotted)

Strip width
Cut to 1½"-wide strips

Tie-Up

	4		
3			
	2		
1			
X		4X	Hem
	X		
	X	5X	
X			
X		6X	
	X		
X			Body of Rug
	X		
X		6X	Hem
	X		
	X	5X	
X			
X		4X	
	X		

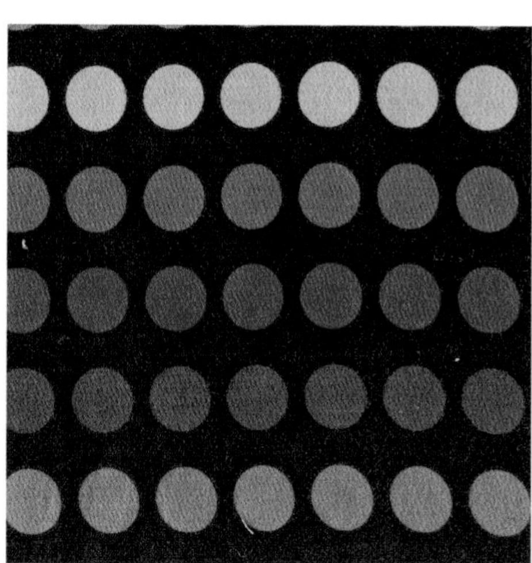

Spice Market

Stripe #1 Warp Faced Stripe (24 EPI)

A				C				A				B				A				C				A			
	A				B				A				C				A				B				A		
		A				C				A				B				A				C				A	
			A				B				A				C				A				B				A
				3X								3X								3X							

Stripe #2 (12 EPI)

F				E				D			
	E				D				F		
		D				F				E	
			F				E				D
← 2X →											

Stripe #3 (12 EPI)

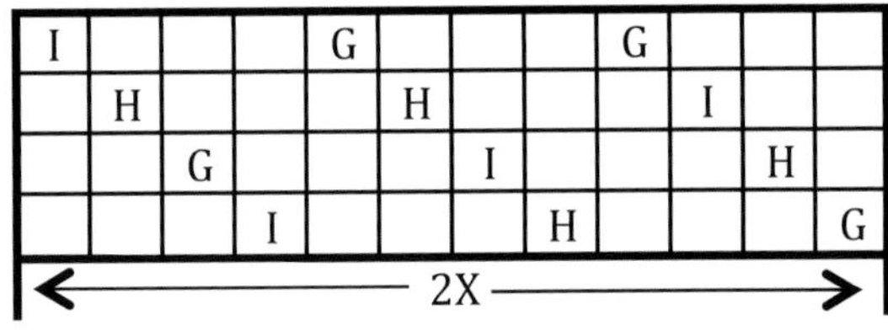

I				G				G			
	H				H				I		
		G				I				H	
			I				H				G
← 2X →											

Stripe Threading Arrangement

#1	#2	#1	#3	#1	#2	#1
Balance			← 3X →			

Tie-Up

	4		
3			
	2		
1			
X		4X	Hem
	X		
	X	5X	
X			
X		6X	
	X		
X		Body of Rug	
	X		
X		6X	Hem
	X		
	X	5X	
X			
X		4X	
	X		

Warp #6

WARP
8/4 Cotton carpet warp

Colors
Black (A)
KY Cardinal (B)
Olive Green (C)
Dark Brown (D)
Rust (E)
Red Brown (F)
Burnt Orange (G)
Bronze Gold (H)
Lime (I)

Sett
12 and 24 EPI
Using a 12-dent reed

Width in Reed
31¼″

WEFT

Hems
2 strands of 8/4 cotton wound together as one

Rug Body
Cotton saris

Strip width
Cut into 3″-wide strips

Sari fabric gives this rug its rich texture

Flannel Nights

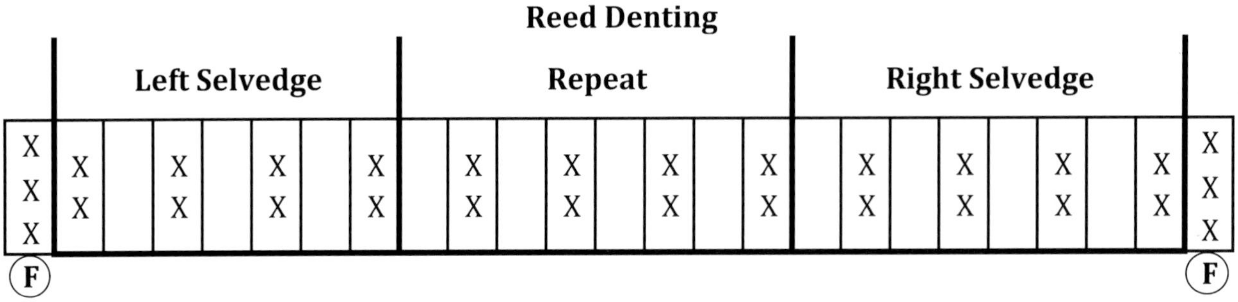

Reed Denting

F	Left Selvedge							Repeat								Right Selvedge								F
X X X	X X		X X		X X		X X		X X		X X		X X		X X		X X		X X		X X		X X	X X X

Threading

4				4				4			
	3				3				3		
		2				2				2	
			1				1				1

Tie-Up

	4	
3		
	2	
1		
X		Heading
	X	
X		Body of Rug
	X	
X		
	X	
X		Heading
	X	

Warp #7

WARP
Fishgarn Size 12/12

Sett
8 EPI (doubled for 4 working EPI)
Use an 8-dent reed and sley for 4 working ends per inch. Thread two ends as one in the heddle eye.

Width in Reed
26"

WEFT

Hem/Header
Use Fishgarn doubled

Rug Body
Cotton flannel
Weave using a temple to avoid draw-in.

Finishing
Full Damascus edge and braided fringe.

Strip width
Cut into 1"-wide strips

Note
F indicates floating selvedge

Leo

Blue Jean Rug

Threading

B				B				B			
	A				A				A		
		B				B				B	
			A				A				A

Tie-Up

	4		4		
3			3		
	2	2			
1		1			
X				4X	Hem
	X				
	X			5X	
X					
X				6X	
	X				
		X		Body of Rug	
			X		
		X			
			X		
X				6X	Hem
	X				
	X			5X	
X					
X				4X	
	X				

Warp #8

WARP

8/4 Cotton carpet warp

Colors

Black (A)

Dark Brown (B)

Sett

16 EPI

2 per dent in an 8-dent reed

Width in Reed

25"

WEFT

Hems

1 strand of black and brown 8/4 cotton wound together as one

Rug Body

Old blue jeans of varying shades

Strip width

Cut into 1"-wide strips, using the length of the leg.

Memories of the Maryland Sheep and Wool Festival

Threading

4				4				4			
	3				3				3		
		2				2				2	
			1				1				1

Tie-Up

	4		4		
3			3		
	2	2			
1		1			
X				4X	Hem
	X				
	X			5X	
X					
X				6X	
	X				
		X			Body of Rug
			X		
		X			
			X		
X				6X	Hem
	X				
	X			5X	
X					
X				4X	
	X				

Warp #9

WARP
8/4 Cotton carpet warp

Color
Linen

Sett
16 EPI
2 per dent in an 8-dent reed

Width in Reed
25"

WEFT

Hems
2 strands of 8/4 cotton wound together as one

Rug Body
Cotton T-shirts

Strip width
Shirts cut horizontally into 1"-wide loops; these were then interlooped to make long lengths of weft.

After many years of attending the festival, I had enough commemorative T-shirts to make rugs in three different color schemes.

Pendleton Wool Blanket Strips 1

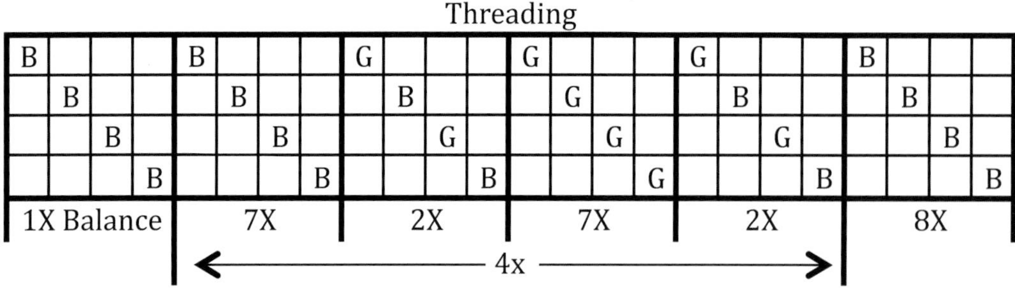

Tie-Up

	4	
3		
	2	
1		
X		4X (Hem)
	X	
	X	5X (Hem)
X		
X		6X (Hem)
	X	
X		Body of Rug
	X	
X		6X (Hem)
	X	
	X	5X (Hem)
X		
X		4X (Hem)
	X	

Warp #10

WARP
8/4 Cotton carpet warp

Colors
Black (B)
Dark Gray (G)

Sett
12 EPI

Width in Reed
27"

WEFT
Hems
2 strands of 8/4 cotton wound together as one

Rug Body
Pendleton fabric strips

Strip width
Precut by manufacturer, aprox. 1" wide

Pendleton Wool Blanket Strips 2

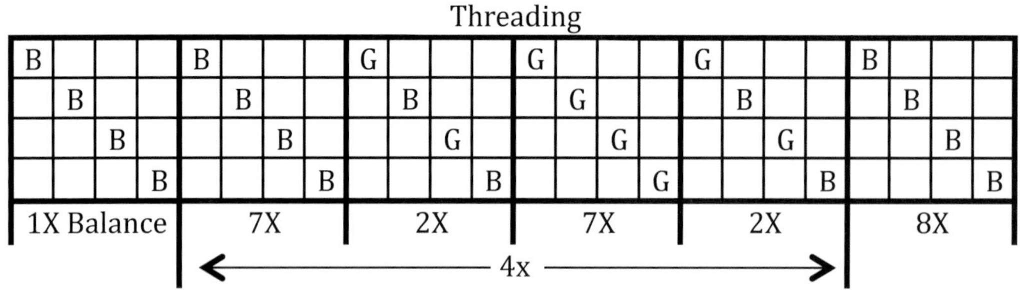

Tie-Up

	4		
3			
	2		
1			
X		4X	Hem
	X		
	X	5X	
X			
X		6X	
	X		
X		Body of Rug	
	X		
X		6X	Hem
	X		
	X	5X	
X			
X		4X	
	X		

Warp #10

WARP
8/4 Cotton carpet warp

Colors
Black (B)
Dark Gray (G)

Sett
12 EPI

Width in Reed
27"

WEFT

Hems
2 strands of 8/4 cotton wound together as one

Rug Body
Pendleton fabric strips

Strip width
Precut by manufacturer, aprox. 1" wide

Coffee Lover's Rug

Center Reverse ↓ … Start ↓

																			2		4		6		8		10	A
										2		4		6		8		10		8		6		4		2		B
	2		4		6		8		10		8		6		4		2											C
10		8		6		4		2																				D

Threading

4			
	3		
		2	
			1

Tie-Up

	4	
3		
	2	
1		
X		4X (Hem)
	X	
	X	5X (Hem)
X		
X		6X (Hem)
	X	
X		Body of Rug
	X	
X		6X (Hem)
	X	
	X	5X (Hem)
X		
X		4X (Hem)
	X	

Warp #11

WARP

8/4 Cotton carpet warp

Colors

Black	(A)	60 ends
Red Brown	(B)	100 ends
Pear	(C)	100 ends
Copper	(D)	50 ends

Sett

12 EPI

Width in Reed

25¾"

WEFT

Hems

2 strands of 8/4 cotton wound together as one

Rug Body

Corduroy

Strip width

Cut into 1½"-wide strips

Painted Desert

Threading

4				4				4			
	3				3				3		
		2				2				2	
			1				1				1

Tie-Up

	4	
3		
	2	
1		
X		4X Heading
	X	
X		Body of Rug
	X	
X		4X Heading
	X	

Warp #12

WARP
8/4 Cotton carpet warp

Color
Copper

Sett
12 EPI

Width in Reed
25"

WEFT
Hems
2 strands of 8/4 cotton wound together as one
8 picks for hem and knotted edge.

Rug Body
Dyed cotton muslin

Strip width
Cut into 1½"-wide strips.
The strips were torn lengthwise from the dyed fabric and woven in sequential order one at a time to allow for a pleasing color transition.

Autumn Stroll

Threading

F				G				F			
	F				G				F		
		F				G				F	
			F				G				F
12X				12X				12X			

← 4X → (repeat of the 2nd and 3rd 12X blocks)

Tie-Up

	4		4		
3			3		
	2	2			
1		1			
X				4X	Hem
	X				
	X			5X	
X					
X				6X	
	X				
		X		Body of Rug	
			X		
		X			
			X		
X				6X	Hem
	X				
	X			5X	
X					
X				4X	
	X				

Warp #13

WARP
8/4 Cotton carpet warp

Colors
Forest (F)
Bronze Gold (G)

Sett
16 EPI

Width in Reed
27"

WEFT
Hems
2 strands of 8/4 cotton wound together as one

Rug Body
Cotton flannel

Strip width
Cut into 1½"-wide strips

Kid's Room

Threading

4				4				4			
	3				3				3		
		2				2				2	
			1				1				1

Tie-Up

	4	
3		
	2	
1		
X		4X
	X	
	X	5X Hem
X		
X		6X
	X	
X		Body of Rug
	X	
X		
	X	
X		6X
	X	
	X	5X Hem
X		
X		4X
	X	

Warp #14

WARP
8/4 Cotton carpet warp

Color
Black

Sett
12 EPI

Width in Reed
24"

WEFT
Hems
2 strands of 8/4 cotton wound together as one

Rug Body
Cotton fabric in bright crayon colors alternating randomly. Cool colors next to warm colors, and light values against dark values.

Strip width
Cut into 1½"-wide strips.

Log Cabin Pattern Thick & Thin

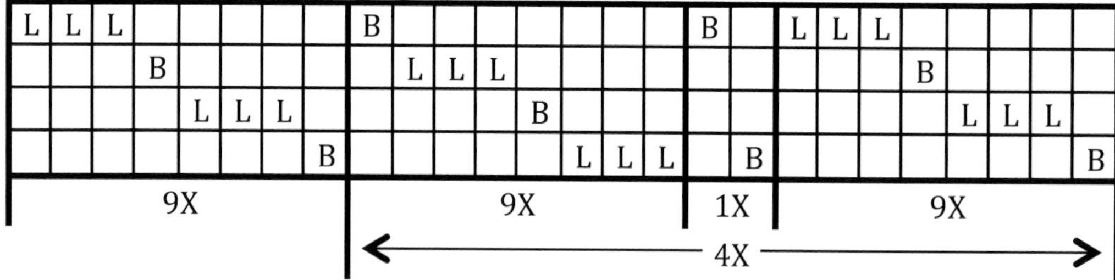

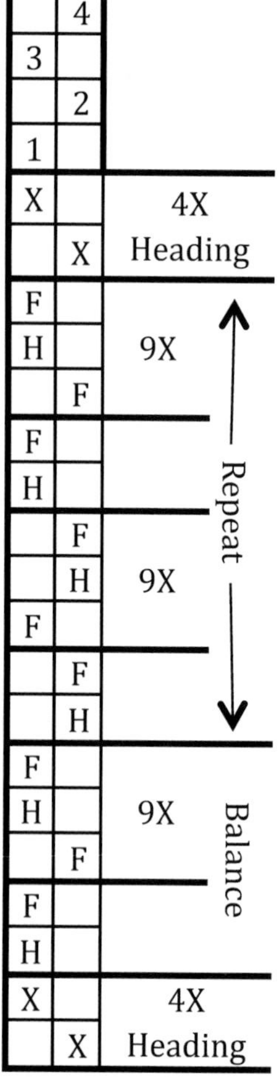

Warp #15

WARP
8/4 carpet warp

Colors
Black (B)
Lime (L)

Sett
24 EPI
2 per dent in a 12-dent reed

Width in Reed
27 1/4"

WEFT

Header
2 strands of 8/4 cotton wound together as one

Rug Body
H = Cotton batik fabric
F = 8/4 carpet warp (black)

Strip width
Cut into 1 1/2"-wide strips

Note
The heavy wefts include a fine weft. The fine weft pick weaves alone.

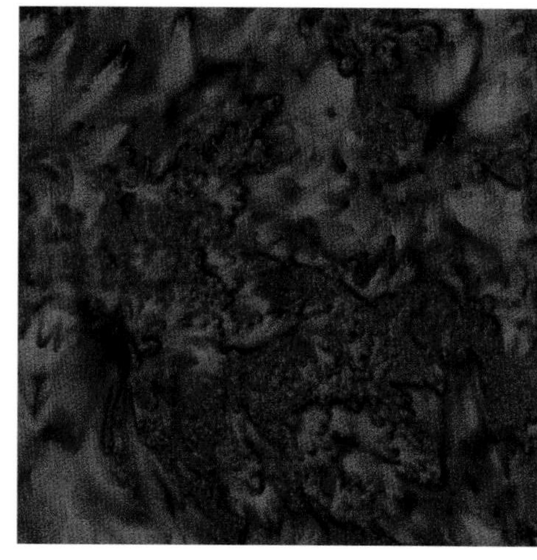

The Zigzag Wool Rug

Threading

4				4				4			
	3				3				3		
		2				2				2	
			1				1				1

Tie-Up

	4	
3		
	2	
1		
X		3X Heading
	X	
X		Body of Rug
R		
	X	
X		
R		
	X	
X		3X Heading
	X	

Warp #16

WARP
3-ply rug wool

Color
Light Gray

Sett
6 EPI

Width in Reed
25"

WEFT
Hems
3-ply rug wool

Rug Body
X = 3-ply rug wool (2 picks)
Note: 2nd pick is shared by wool strip of fabric.
R = Pendleton wool strips with colored stripes

Strip width
Precut from manufacturer, aprox. 1" wide
The colored stripes are laid in and each successive weft strip is shifted to create the zigzag pattern.

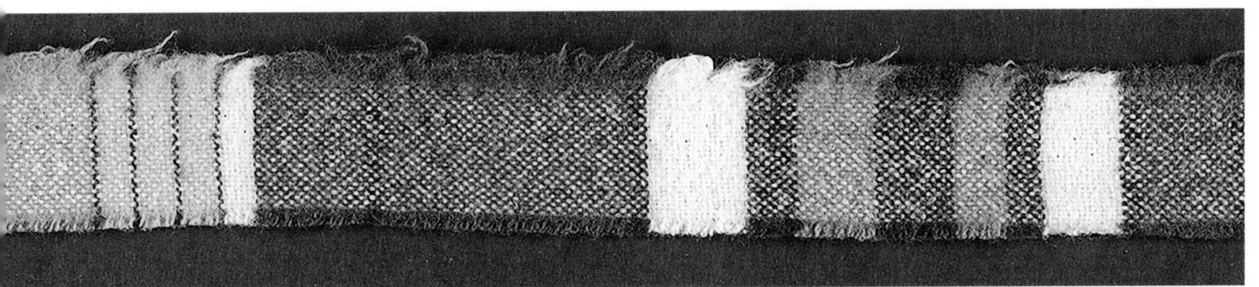

Warm and Cool

Threading

4				4				4			
	3				3				3		
		2				2				2	
			1				1				1

Tie-Up

	4		
3			
	2		
1			
X		4X	Hem
	X		
	X	5X	
X			
X		6X	
	X		
X			Body of Rug
	X		
X			
	X		
X		6X	Hem
	X		
	X	5X	
X			
X		4X	
	X		

Warp #17

WARP
8/4 carpet warp

Color
Black

Sett
12 EPI

Width in Reed
26"

WEFT

Hems
2 strands of 8/4 cotton wound together as one

Rug Body
Dyed silk fabric

Strip width
Cut into 1½"-wide strips

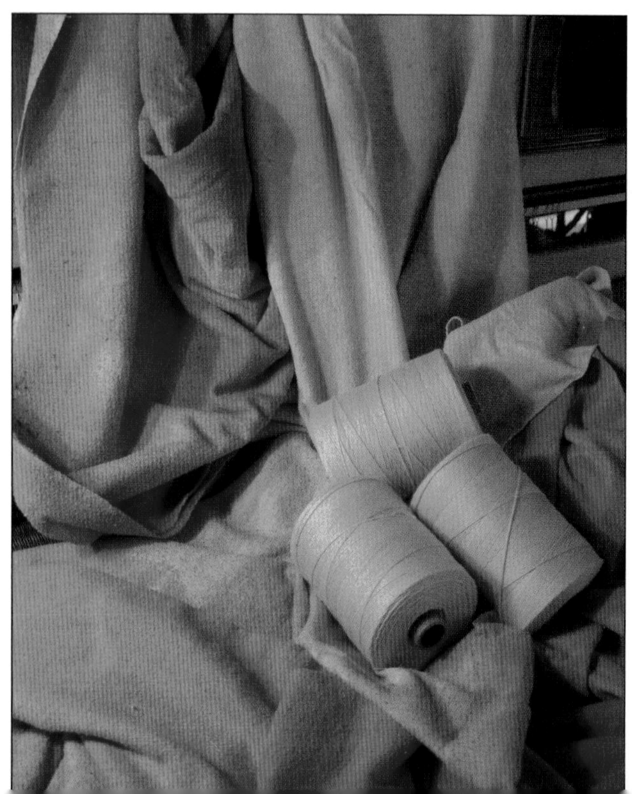

Mushroom Foray

Threading

T				B				D			
	B				D				T		
		D				T				B	
			T				B				D

← 26X →

Tie-Up

	4		
3			
	2		
1			
X		4X	Hem
	X		
	X	5X	
X			
X		6X	
	X		
X		Body of Rug	
	X		
X			
	X		
X		6X	Hem
	X		
	X	5X	
X			
X		4X	
	X		

Warp #17

WARP
8/4 carpet warp

Colors
Dark Brown (D)
Red Brown (B)
Tan (T)

Sett
12 EPI

Width in Reed
26"

WEFT
Hems
2 strands of 8/4 cotton wound together as one

Rug Body
Dyed silk fabric

Strip width
Cut into 1½"-wide strips

Rose Path Twill

	Border																								Border			
				4				4		4				4				4		4				4				
			3				3				3						3				3				3			
		2				2						2				2						2				2		
F	1				1				1				1		1				1				1				1	F
	1X				Balance Last Time									19X										1X				

Tie-Up

	4	4	4		
3		3			3
	2			2	2
1			1	1	

X						4X Heading
	X					
		X				Body of Rug
			X			
				X		
					X	
		X				
					X	
				X		
			X			
		X				
					X	
				X		
					X	
		X				Last time to Balance
			X			
				X		
					X	
		X				
					X	
				X		
			X			
		X				
X						4X Heading
	X					

Warp #18

WARP
8/4 carpet warp

Color
Colonial Green

Sett
16 EPI (8 working EPI)
Thread two ends as one.
Note: Use floating selvedges

Width in Reed
26"

WEFT

Hems
2 strands of 8/4 cotton wound together as one

Rug Body
Cotton print fabric

Strip width
Cut into 1½"-wide strips

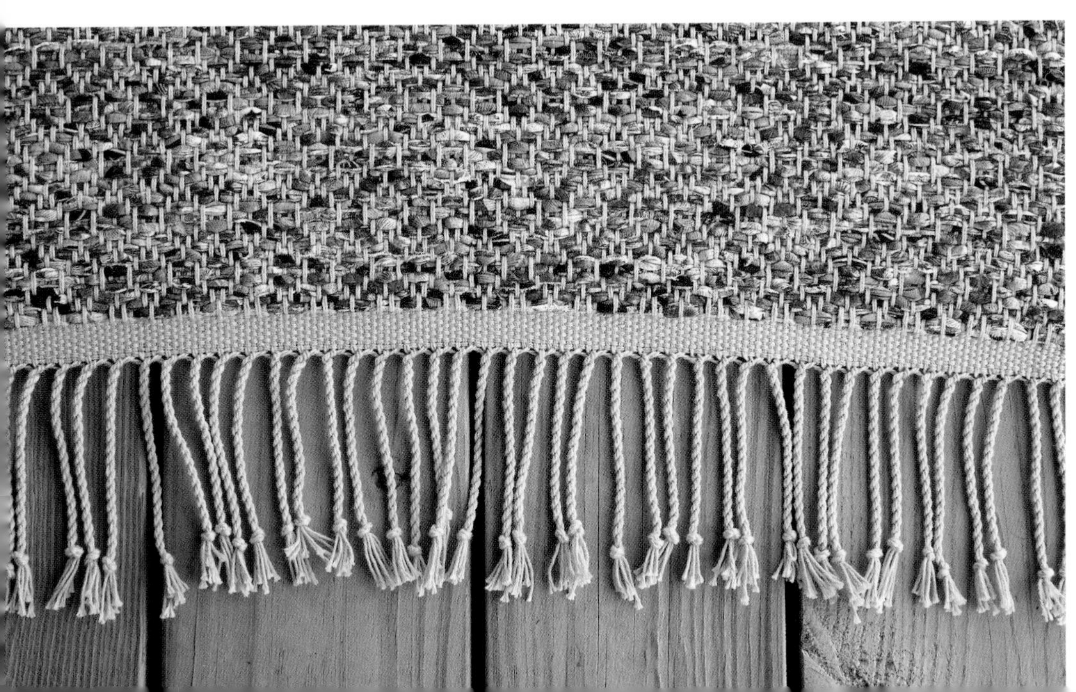

Anderson in Corduroy

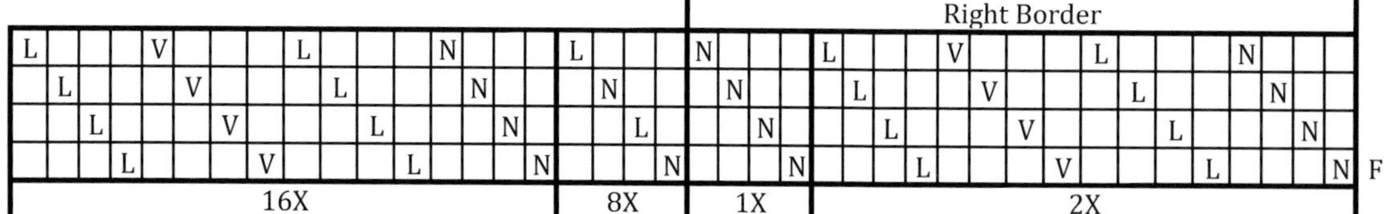

Left Border

F 1X 2X 8X 1X

Tie-Up

Hem 4X 5X 6X

Body of Rug

6X 5X 4X Hem

Warp #19

WARP
8/4 carpet warp

Colors
Navy (N)
Limestone (L)
Velvet (V)

Sett
16 EPI

Width in Reed
24.75"

WEFT

Hems
2 strands of 8/4 cotton wound together as one

Rug Body
Corduroy

Strip width
Cut into 1½"-wide strips

Violet Anderson

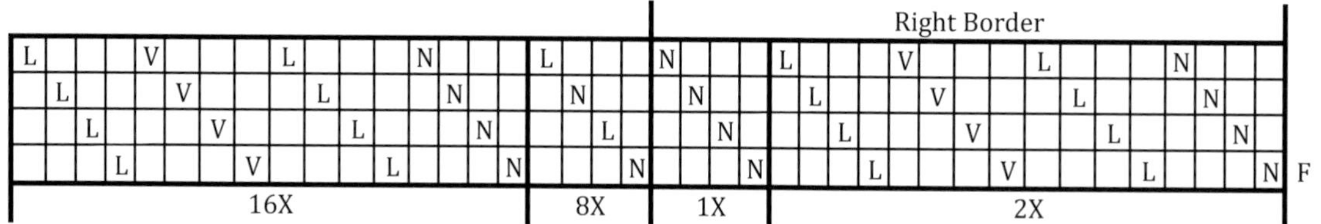

Left Border

N				L				V				L				N				L				N			
	N				L				V				L				N				N				N		
		N				L				V				L				N				L				N	
			N				L				V				L				N				N				N
F 1X				2X																8X				1X			

Tie-Up

		4	4		4	
	3	3		3		
2	2				2	
1			1	1		F
				X		4X Hem
					X	
					X	5X Hem
				X		
				X		6X Hem
					X	
X						Body of Rug
	X					
		X				
			X			
X						
			X			
		X				
	X					
				X		6X Hem
					X	
					X	5X Hem
				X		
				X		4X Hem
					X	

Warp #19

WARP
8/4 carpet warp

Colors
Navy (N)
Limestone (L)
Velvet (V)

Sett
16 EPI

Width in Reed
24¾"

WEFT

Hems
2 strands of 8/4 cotton wound together as one

Rug Body
Solid poly-cotton-blend fabric

Strip width
Cut into 1½"-wide strips

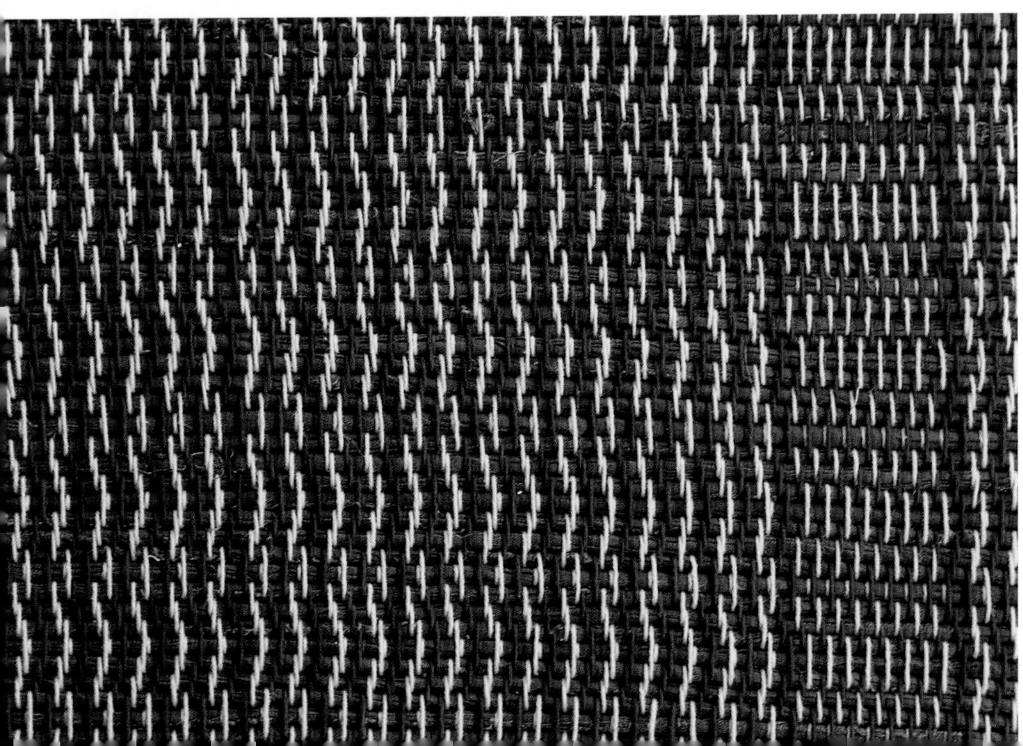

Plaid Anderson

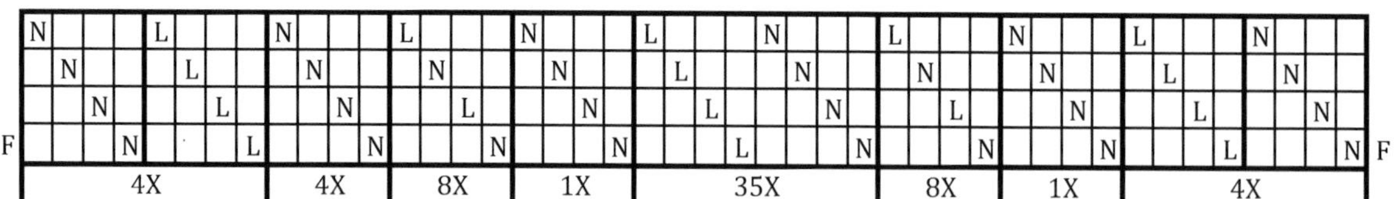

Tie-Up

4X
5X
6X
Hem

Body of Rug

6X
5X
4X
Hem

Warp #20

WARP
8/4 carpet warp

Colors
Dark Navy (N)
Limestone (L)

Sett
16 EPI

Width in Reed
26¼"

WEFT

Hems
2 strands of 8/4 cotton wound together as one

Rug Body
Cotton flannel fabric

Strip width
Cut into 1½"-wide strips

Welcome to Hollywood

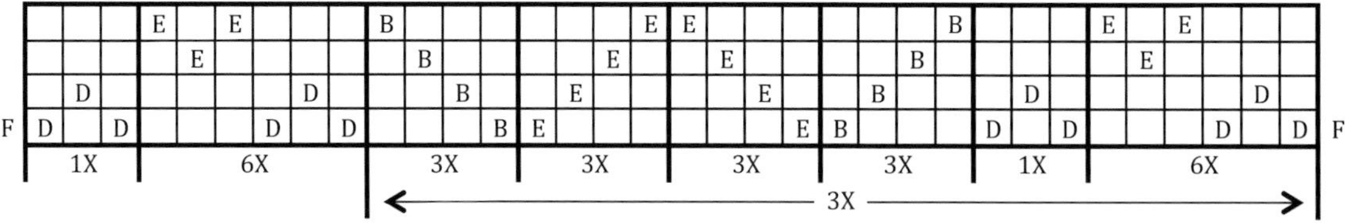

Tie-Up

		4	4		4		
	3	3		3			
2	2				2		
1			1	1			
				X		4X	Hem
					X		
					X	5X	
				X			
				X		6X	
					X		
X						Body of Rug	
	X						
		X					
			X				
				X		6X	Hem
					X		
					X	5X	
				X			
				X		4X	
					X		

Warp #21

This pattern has been known for years as the Hollywood Pattern and is a combination of the Double Seed Stitch and Point Twill patterns. The Hollywood Pattern was offered in the instruction booklet from the Newcomb Loom Co. The double ends at the points are not a mistake but done intentionally.

WARP
8/4 carpet warp

Colors
Dark Brown (D)
Ecru (E)
Black (B)

Sett
12 EPI

Width in Reed
25"

WEFT
Hems
2 strands of 8/4 cotton wound together as one

Rug Body
Wool blend fabric

Strip width
Cut into 1½"-wide strips

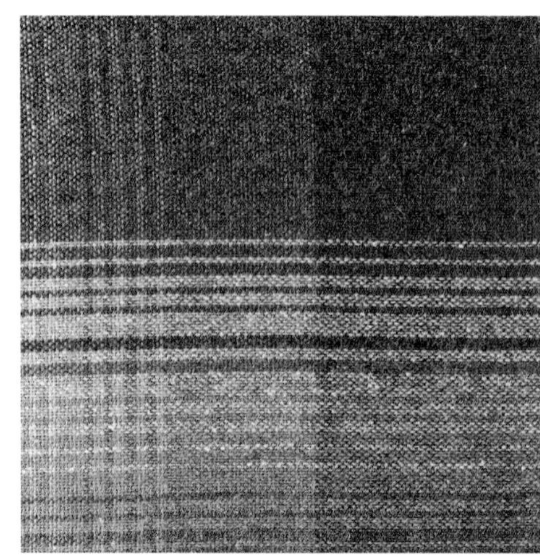

Chicken Tracks

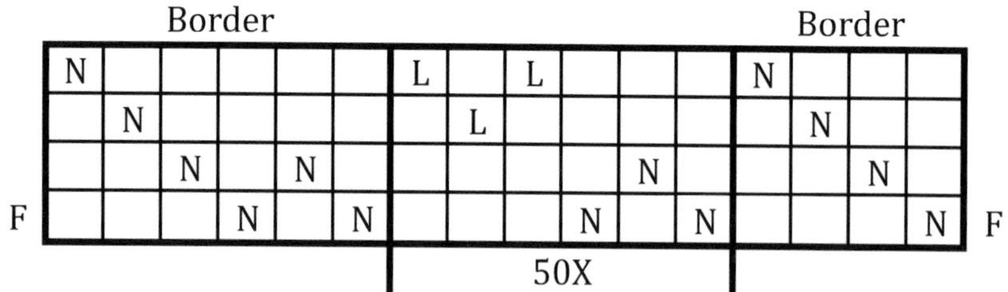

Tie-Up

		4	4		4	
	3	3		3		
2	2				2	
1			1	1		
				X		4X Heading
					X	
X						Body of Rug
	X					
		X				
			X			
				X		4X Heading
					X	

Warp #22

WARP
8/4 carpet warp

Colors
Navy (N)
Limestone (L)

Sett
12 EPI

Width in Reed
26"

WEFT
Hems
2 strands of 8/4 cotton wound together as one

Rug Body
Cotton fabric

Strip width
Cut into 1½"-wide strips

A Whole Flock of Chickens

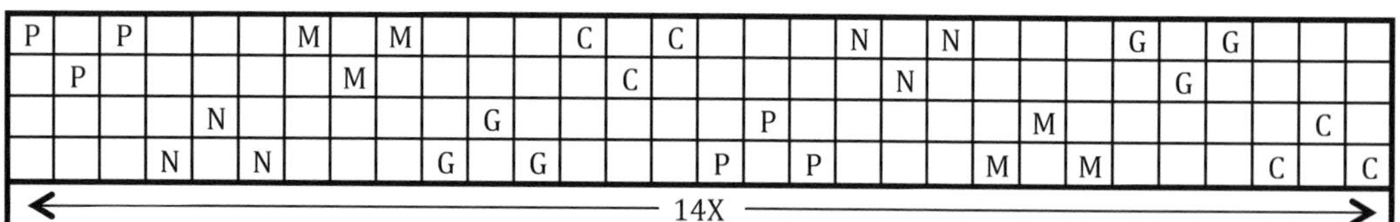

1	2	3	4	5	6	7	8	9	10	11	12	13	14	15	16	17	18	19	20	21	22	23	24	25	26	27	28	29	30
P		P				M		M				C		C				N		N				G		G			
	P						M						C						N						G				
				N						G						P						M						C	
			N		N				G		G				P		P				M		M				C		C

← 14X →

Tie-Up

		4	4		4	
	3	3		3		
2	2				2	
1			1	1		
				X		4X Heading
					X	
X						Body of Rug
	X					
		X				
			X			
				X		4X Heading
					X	

Warp #23

WARP
8/4 carpet warp

Colors
KY Cardinal (C)
Gold (G)
Myrtle Green (M)
Navy Blue (N)
Parakeet (P)

Sett
16 EPI

Width in Reed
26¼"

WEFT
Hems
2 strands of 8/4 cotton wound together as one

Rug Body
Cotton fabric

Strip width
Cut into 1½"-wide strips

Two-Sided Broken Twill Rug

Threading

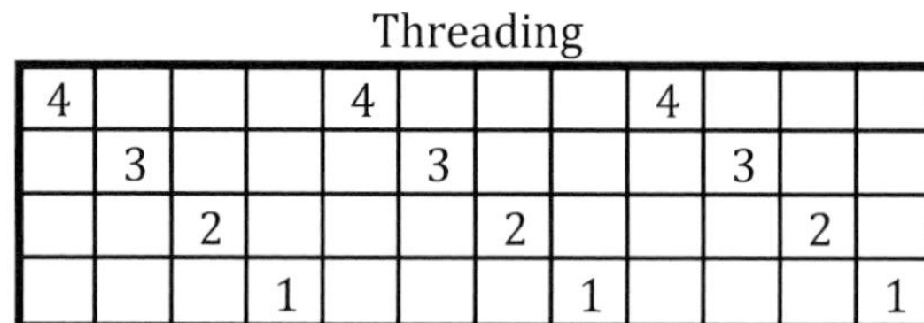

4				4				4			
	3				3				3		
		2				2				2	
			1				1				1

Direct Tie-Up

			4		
		3			
	2				
1					
X		X		4X	Hem
	X		X		
	X		X	5X	
X		X			
X		X		6X	
	X		X		
A				Body of Rug	
B	B	B			
		A			
B		B	B		
	A				
B	B		B		
			A		
	B	B	B		
X		X		6X	Hem
	X		X		
	X		X	5X	
X		X			
X		X		4X	
	X		X		

Warp #24

WARP
8/4 carpet warp

Color
Dark Brown

Sett
12 EPI

Width in Reed
26"

WEFT

Hems
2 strands of 8/4 cotton wound together as one

Rug Body
Two different colors of cotton fabric

Strip width
Cut into 1"-wide strips
A Weaves top layer
B Weaves bottom layer

Ms & Os

	Right Selvedge				B Block															A Block															Left Selvedge				
		4		4	4		4				4		3				4		4				4		4				4		4				4		4		
						3						3						3			3						3						3						
									2						2									2						2									
F	1		1					1		1				1		1				1		1				1		1				1		1		1		1	F

12X (B Block and A Block)

Balance Last Time (A Block)

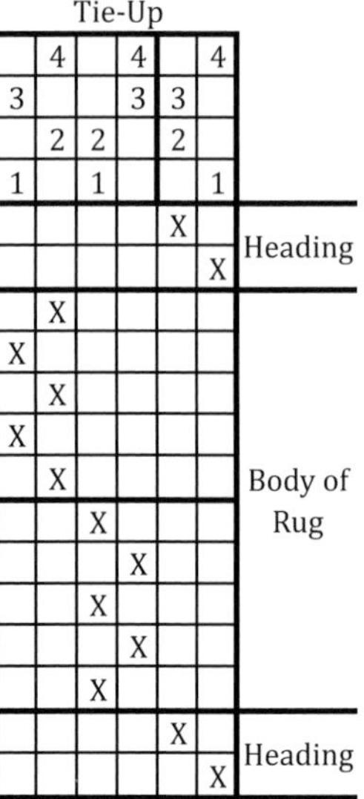

Warp #25

WARP
8/4 carpet warp

Color
Dark Brown

Sett
15 EPI

Width in Reed
25.5"

WEFT

Hems
2 strands of 8/4 cotton wound together as one

Rug Body
Cotton fabric

Strip width
Cut into 1½"-wide strips

Thread blocks A and B, repeating them 12 times, then ending with an A block.

Note
Use two ends of 8/4 cotton for floating selvedges.

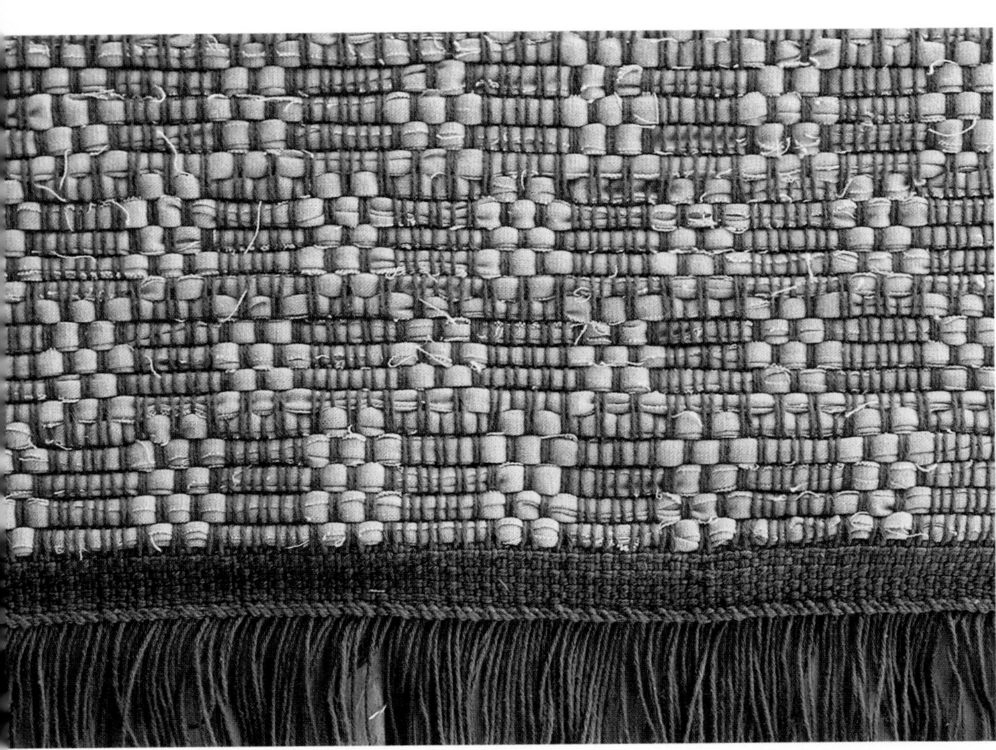

Gamps

A gamp is another word for a sampler. It is made up of a number of different elements all in one piece—instead of weaving dozens and dozens of individual test rugs made up of one warp and one weft, you can combine the colors you want to test in a single rug. For each of the gamps shown here, I warped a loom with several stripes in a particular color family: one rug in neutral colors, another in reds and purples, another in yellows and oranges, and the last in blues and greens. In each of these warps, I wove 15 different colored stripes (the same 15 colors in each rug). Looking closely at the rugs this process produced, you can see how the same weft color looks different with different warp colors. Gamps like these allow me to quickly see how different colors will interact with each other and to decide whether I would like them together in a larger (and higher-commitment) project. A 3-by-3-inch square that I love is more valuable to me than a 3-by-5-foot rug that I dislike.

All four rugs were made with the same fabric strips and basic threading draft.

WARP
8/4 carpet warp

Sett
12 EPI

Width in Reed
28"

WEFT
Hems
2 strands of 8/4 cotton wound together as one

Rug Body
Cotton fabric

Strip width
Cut into 1½"-wide strips

The Rag Colors

The only difference between the four rugs is the colors of warp thread.

Gamp #1: The Neutrals

Black				Dk Grey				White				Ivory				Ecru				Red Brown				Dk Brown			
4				4				4				4				4				4				4			
	3				3				3				3				3				3				3		
		2				2				2				2				2				2				2	
			1				1				1				1				1				1				1
12X				12X				12X				12X				12X				12X				12X			

Tie-Up

	4
3	
	2
1	

X		4X	Hem
	X		
	X	5X	
X			
X		6X	
	X		
X		Black	
	X		
X		Grey	
	X		
X		White	
	X		
X		Yellow	
	X		
X		Yellow Orange	
	X		
X		Orange	
	X		
X		Red Orange	
	X		
X		Red	
	X		
X		Red Violet	
	X		
X		Violet	
	X		
X		Blue Violet	
	X		
X		Blue	
	X		
X		Blue Green	
	X		
X		Green	
	X		
X		Yellow Green	
	X		
X		6X	Hem
	X		
	X	5X	
X			
X		4X	
	X		

Colors
Black
Dark Grey
White
Ivory or Natural
Ecru
Red Brown
Dark Brown

Gamp #4: Blues & Greens

Navy				Royal				Slate				Colonial Green				Myrtle				Forest			
4				4				4				4				4				4			
	3				3				3				3				3				3		
		2				2				2				2				2				2	
			1				1				1				1				1				1
12X				12X				12X				12X				12X				12X			

Tie-Up

	4
3	
	2
1	

X		4X	Hem
	X		
	X	5X	
X			
X		6X	
	X		
X		Black	
	X		
X		Grey	
	X		
X		White	
	X		
X		Yellow	
	X		
X		Yellow Orange	
	X		
X		Orange	
	X		
X		Red Orange	
	X		
X		Red	
	X		
X		Red Violet	
	X		
X		Violet	
	X		
X		Blue Violet	
	X		
X		Blue	
	X		
X		Blue Green	
	X		
X		Green	
	X		
X		Yellow Green	
	X		
X		6X	Hem
	X		
	X	5X	
X			
X		4X	
	X		

Colors
Navy Blue
Royal Blue
Slate Grey
Colonial Green
Myrtle Green
Forest Green

Acknowledgments

This book is only possible because of the help of so many people. I want to thank Debra Smith and Stackpole Books for asking me to write this book. Debra is a former weaving student of mine who loves weaving and rags maybe nearly as much as I do. Her love for little bits of wool rags and the whole idea of recycling has led her to become the editor of *Rug Hooking Magazine*. Good job Debra!

Thanks go to Carol and Ron Woolcock, the owners of The Mannings Handweaving School and Supply Center. We have worked hard together over the past three decades to create a school and environment where students can learn about textiles of all kinds—and most of all, become longtime friends. Thank you for your trust and believing in what I bring to the studio and classroom.

Thanks also go to all my students, who have taught me more than they will ever know. So, so many of you are like family to me and I will love you forever. From you, I have learned so much—how to be patient, how to describe a situation or answer a question half a dozen different ways. You have taught me that nothing in weaving is wrong; it just maybe could be done differently. Mishaps are nothing more than opportunities to learn something. A broken warp

Just some of the people who helped me weave all those rugs. *From left to right:* Careena Emrich, Tom Knisely, Schelly Reynolds, Amanda Robinet, Susan Kesler Simpson, Heather Watts, Vonnie Davis, and Leslie Deardorff. *Not pictured:* Joanne Trygg, Brenda Kuyper, Kathleen Eckhaus, Sara Bixler and Judah Emrich.

thread or rough selvedge is nothing to lose sleep over: Observe, don't ever be afraid to ask a question, then laugh and then move on. But always laugh.

Debra Smith was brilliant when she suggested that I recruit some of my students to help me weave some of the rugs that you see here in the book. When asked, each and every one of them eagerly jumped at the idea to help me. Using my designs and colorways, each person went home with spools of thread and bolts of fabric, eager to help with this project, and for that I am forever grateful. I couldn't have done this book in such a timely manner without all of you. The people who helped me with all of this weaving are Sara Bixler, Vonnie Davis, Leslie Deardorff, Kathleen Eckhaus, Careena Emrich, Judah Emrich, Brenda Kuyper, Schelly Reynolds, Amanda Robinet, Susan Kesler Simpson, Joanne Trygg, and Heather Watts.

Thank you to Sandy Morales for all the trips to Pendleton Woolen Mill to pick out wool rag strips for me and then sending them on for us to weave.

When I put the word out that I was looking for older Maryland Sheep and Wool Festival T-Shirts for a rag rug, so many people went through their closets and donated. Thanks to all of you.

I had thought about writing a book for a very long time, but the timing was never quite right until now. The responsibilities of work, maintaining a property, and, most importantly, my family were always first on my mind. But the dynamics of life change, the right time came, and I took full advantage of it. Thank you, Susan Gettys, for pointing this out and being such a good sounding board for me. Hugs to you.

I close this with a heartfelt thank you to my family for being encouraging and supportive throughout the years. You never thought my work was without meaning and you always encouraged me to keep doing the thing I love most, weaving. Thank you Charlotte, Sara, Hannah, Olivia, Dustin, and Vishal. I love you all.

Sara, my daughter and friend. Thank you for taking all my hand-drawn threading drafts and making them more legible for the publisher, checking over them, and making sure that they were consistent and made sense to the readers. When you were all done typing them and helping me to meet the schedule for the publisher you asked me, "Alright Dad, where do we go from here—and what's next? Another book?" I love you, honey. You really know me.

A final and very special thank you to my cousin Nancy Fallen. Years ago, Nancy encouraged me to start writing a book. A published author of textbooks herself, Nancy told me to start my day with an hour of writing and, day by day, I would soon get it done. You were so right, Nancy, and I thank you for your wise advice. I did it!

Glossary

Apron bar. A wood or metal rod to which the warp is tied, either on the front or back of the loom.

Back beam. The beam located in the back of the loom that provides a stable surface for the warp to travel over as it comes up from the warp beam and moves toward the harness frames.

Barn frame. The timber frames used in looms of the past.

Beaming. The process of winding the warp onto the warp beam of the loom.

Beater. The frame that holds the reed and swings forward to beat the weft materials against the fell. The beater can swing from overhead or be underslung and attached to the frame of the loom at the bottom of the loom's frame.

Bobbin. A small tube with flanges on the sides that you wind finer weft threads onto. The bobbin is placed into a shuttle.

Brake. The device located on the warp beam that holds tension on the warp as you weave.

Breast beam. The beam located in the front of the loom that provides a stable surface for the woven fabric to pass over on its way to the cloth beam. Also known as the front beam.

Castle. The portion of the loom that holds the harness frames.

Cloth beam. The beam located in the front of the loom that holds the finished woven fabric as you weave.

Counterbalance loom. A loom where the harness frames are suspended from rollers by cables or ropes that allow the harness frames to move both up and down, providing a large shed.

Dent. The open space in the reed between the teeth.

Draft. The illustrated recipe that describes the threading order and treadling order of a pattern.

EPI. The abbreviation for ends per inch.

Ends. Individual threads.

Fell. The last row or pick of the woven fabric.

Harness. The framework that holds the heddles and moves the warp to create the opening for the shuttle to pass through. Also known as the shaft.

Heading. The beginning and ending portion of a piece of fabric or rug. It provides a stable place to tie knots against or can be woven wider and rolled into a hem.

Heddle. The wire or cord guides for the warp threads. Heddles are located on the harness frame or shaft and slide from side to side; each heddle has an eye through which a warp end is threaded.

Jack loom. A type of loom where the harness frames move upward to create the shed. A jack loom is also known as a rising-shed loom.

Lams. Wooden slats located underneath the harness frames, to which the treadles are attached. There is a lam for each harness on a loom.

Lease sticks. Smooth, finished wooden sticks that are placed into the warp to help maintain the cross in a warp.

Loom. A framework that holds the warp threads under even tension as you weave.

Mill. A vertical frame that spins back and forth and measures the warp length. Also known as a warping reel.

Pawl. The catch lever that, used in conjunction with a ratchet located on the cloth beam holds the tension on the warp. Also known as a "dog."

Pick. A weft row or even shot.

Plain beam. A warp beam that is flat and uses sticks or corrugated cardboard or paper between the layers of warp to maintain an even tension.

Ratchet. A device that, in conjunction with the pawl, holds the tension on the warp. The rachet is a round metal disk with teeth cut along the circumference to allow the pawl or dog to engage, located on the cloth beam. Some looms have a second rachet on the warp beam.

Reed. This comblike device spaces the warp threads to a certain density or ends per inch. It is placed in the beater and is also used to push the weft material back against the fell of the fabric when the beater is brought forward.

Selvedge. The edge of the woven material.

Sett. The ends per inch (EPI) in a rug.

Shed. The opening made in front of the reed when the treadles are pushed and the harnesses move. This opening is where the shuttle is tossed from side to side.

Shot. A single row of weft. Also known as a pick.

Shuttle. The piece of wood that is wound with the weft material and carries the weft from selvedge to selvedge as you weave.

Shuttle race. The part of the beater assembly that acts like a ledge to support the shuttle as you weave.

Sley. The process of placing the warp threads through the dents in the reed.

Sley hook or sleying hook. A small metal or plastic S-shaped hook used to pull the warp through the dents in a reed. Also known as a reed hook.

Temple. An adjustable stretcher, made of metal or wood with sharp stainless-steel teeth at each end, that is used to avoid excess draw-in as you weave.

Tie-up. The connection of the treadles to the harness frames. The tie-up in a weaving draft is usually the box to the right of the threading; it illustrates which harness frames get tied to which treadle.

Treadle. The peddles located under the loom to which the harness frames are attached.

Warp. The threads that make up the foundation of the rug or fabric. These threads are located on the loom.

Warp beam. The beam in the back of the loom that the warp is wound onto to be stored.

Warp-faced rug. A rug or fabric where the warp threads are sleyed closely together, preventing the weft from being visible except at the selvedge edge, where the weft turns back on itself.

Warping board. A sturdy frame, usually constructed of wood with wooden pegs extending out from it, which provide a way of measuring out the length of thread needed to make a warp.

Weft. The material wound onto the shuttle and woven horizontally from selvedge to selvedge.

Weft-faced rug. A rug or fabric where the warp is sleyed coarsely in the reed. This allows the weft materials to slide down and cover the warp completely. Tapestries and Navajo rugs are well-known examples of weft-faced rugs.

Bibliography

Here are some books and periodicals that I feel will be helpful to you as you continue to weave rag rugs.

Allen, Heather. *Weaving Contemporary Rag Rugs: New Designs, Traditional Techniques.* Asheville, NC: Lark Books, 2001.

Baizerman, Suzanne, and Karen Searle. *Finishes in the Ethnic Tradition.* Dos Tejedoras Fiber Arts Publications, 1989.

Burnham, Harold B., and Dorothy K. Burnham. *Keep Me Warm One Night: Early Handweaving in Eastern Canada.* Toronto: University of Toronto Press in cooperation with the Royal Ontario Museum, 1975.

Collingwood, Peter. *The Techniques of Rug Weaving.* New York: Watson-Guptill, 1950.

Chandler, Debra. *Learning to Weave.* Loveland, CO: Interweave Press, 1995.

Davison, Marguerite Porter. *A Handweaver's Pattern Book.* 1950

Erickson, Johanna. *Rag Rug Gimmicks and Tricks.* Self-published, 1999.

Gordon, Beverly. *Shaker Textile Arts.* Hanover, NH: University Press of New England, 1980.

Handwoven Magazine. Loveland, CO: Interweave Press.

Knisely, Tom. *A Comprehensive Guide to Warping Your Loom Front to Back.* DVD. East Berlin, PA: The Mannings Handweaving School and Supply Center, 2004.

———. *A Loom Owner's Companion.* DVD. Loveland, CO: Interweave Press, 2011.

———. *Weave a Good Rug.* DVD. Loveland, CO: Interweave Press, 2012.

Ligon, Linda Collier. *A Rug Weaver's Source Book.* Loveland, CO: Interweave Press, 1984.

Meany, Janet, and Paula Pfaff. *Rag Rug Handbook.* Loveland, CO: Interweave Press, 1996. Originally published by Dos Tejedoras Fiber Arts Publications, 1985.

Montgomery, Florence M. *Textiles in America, 1650-1870.* New York: W. W. Norton & Company, 2007.

Wieand, Paul R. "Carpet-Rag Parties." *Pennsylvania Folklife Magazine* Vol. 46 No. 3 (Spring 1997).

Yoshida, Shin-Ichiro, and Dai Williams. *Riches from Rags: Saki-ori & Other Recycling Traditions in Japanese Rural Clothing.* San Francisco: San Francisco Craft and Folk Art Museum, 1994.

Notes

Notes

Notes

Notes